SHOTGUN
Weddings

SHOTGUN
Weddings

THE SAGA OF GRANDMA COKEY, CALIFORNIA'S SERIAL HUSBAND KILLER

LLOYD BILLINGSLEY

A Centershot Book

Also by Lloyd Billingsley

Exceptional Depravity: Dan Who Likes Dark and Double Murder in Davis, California

Hollywood Party: Stalinist Adventures in the American Movie Industry

ISBN 978-0-9968581-0-6 (pbk.)

Second edition 2016

Printed in the United States of America

1 2 3 4 5 6 7 8 9 10

For FLB

A man's foes shall be they of his own household.

-- Matthew 10:36

"She killed him, didn't she?"

On January 7, 2013, a chilly Monday morning during a particularly cold month in Los Angeles, detective Pamela Stirling reported for duty at the Police Administrative Building, also known as the PAB and the "Chief's Building," at 100 West First Street. Stirling worked in the PAB as adjutant to LAPD Captain William Hayes in the robbery-homicide division. A casual observer, in or outside of the department, might assume that the slender blond had perhaps taken a shortcut to that job. The observer would be wrong.

Pamela Stirling came up through Mercy High, an all-girls Catholic school in the state capital of Sacramento, where she competed in gymnastics. Then it was on to Sacramento State, Santa Monica College and Chapman University, criminal justice major. Stirling entered the police academy at 22 and promptly joined the LAPD. Her beats included West Los Angeles and bike patrol near the University of Southern California, a top-drawer school in a decidedly dangerous neighborhood. After working undercover in vice for more than two years, she qualified as a detective, then as a detective supervisor. After assignment to the Sexual Assault Section, she worked briefly with the Cold Case Homicide Division before becoming the captain's adjutant in the Robbery-Homicide Division. By any standard, the mother of three had paid her dues.

Midway through the morning, Captain Hayes called Stirling into his office.

The detective did not find it unusual that her boss would want to talk something over. California's largest city, after all, suffers no shortage of robbery or homicide. The vast city had seen the Manson murders, the Angelo Buono and Kenneth Bianchi "Hillside Strangler," tandem, the "Night Stalker," Richard Ramirez, the O.J. Simpson case and many others. For robbery and overall mayhem, nothing tops the L.A. riots in 1992, with some 11,000 arrests and National Guard troops in the streets.

As in many American cities, police in Los Angeles remain under heavy scrutiny from those whose concern for the rights of violent criminals surpasses the rights of their victims. It was not out of the question that Stirling had run afoul of some unwritten law or become the target of politically correct zealotry. When Hayes closed the door behind her, she saw that detective Carla Zuniga was also present in the office. Stirling found nothing strange about that, except that her colleague and close friend was standing there crying. Stirling felt a sharp stab of panic.

"Are my children okay?" she asked. "Is my husband okay?"

The faces of Hayes and Zuniga told her it was not her kids, or her husband.

"It's my dad," Stirling said. "She killed him, didn't she?"

It was not really a question. Deep inside, a voice was saying, "I just knew it." And she was right. It was her dad. The meeting in Hayes' office ended quickly.

Detective Rob Marion drove Stirling to the Temple Street office of her husband Phillip Stirling, a Los Angeles deputy district attorney she met in a 1996 homicide trial. The couple drove home, packed up their suitcases, headed to the Burbank airport and hopped a flight to the state capital of Sacramento. They spent the night with Pam's brother Andy and his wife Michelle in Grass Valley, in the Sierra foothills to the east. In the morning they drove south to Placerville to meet with El Dorado County deputy district attorney Joe Alexander and investigator Joe Ramsey. Southeast of town, at 3248 Wilderness Court, LAPD detective Pamela Stirling witnessed the crime scene.

Her father, Robert Edward Harris, was a retired U.S. Forest service supervisor. While asleep or resting in the bedroom, the 72-year-old had been shot in the head, by all appearances, with a 12-gauge shotgun. Pamela Stirling was no stranger to crime scenes and gun violence but in her long experience she had never seen anything quite like this, and nothing remotely similar involving a family member. The shotgun blast had left blood spatter on the ceiling, and someone had made an effort to clean it up, with little success, leaving only smears. On the other hand, nobody had attempted to clean up the blood, brain matter and flesh from a chair, a pillow, the headboard, bedding and the ceiling fan. Pamela Stirling, the victim's daughter, witnessed the scene with a sense of horror.

As she learned, on January 6, a local attorney named David Weiner had called 911, and El Dorado County dispatchers then called Colleen Harris, 70, Robert Harris' wife. She told dispatchers everything was okay and she was there by herself. Dispatchers posed other pertinent questions but received no clear answers.

When deputies arrived, they saw Colleen Harris moving about the Wilderness Court house conducting what they described as normal household activities. She told the deputies her husband Bob Harris had been shot and was dead. She explained that the weapon was next to him on the bed, but that she did not know what kind of gun it was. As deputies learned, the weapon was a double-barreled 12-gauge shotgun, with shortened barrels and stock.

Colleen Harris refused to say if she had shot Bob Harris, her third husband. She did tell police she thought he had a nosebleed, that she had covered him with a blanket, and that he had not moved.

"He looks so beautiful," she told deputies, weeping. Beyond that, deputies said, she showed no sign of distress, and at one point even started joking around.

For her part, LAPD detective Pamela Stirling experienced plenty of distress after witnessing the crime scene and learning the facts.

It was her dad, she did kill him, and the detective "just knew it." Pamela Stirling also knew something else of considerable significance.

Nearly 30 years before, Colleen killed her second husband. She killed him with a shotgun. She killed him in the bedroom of the house they shared. And as the grieving detective also knew, the similarities did not end there.

"I think I shot my husband."

The woman who had killed Bob Harris was born in San Francisco on March 28, 1942, daughter of Irwin "Irish" Yates, who ran a liquor store in nearby Richmond. Colleen Yates had two siblings, Sharon and Michael, and after high school Colleen attended nursing school in Montana. As she told a longtime friend, while at nursing school she lived with a Dr. Charles Dodge, whose wife was a nurse in the hospital where Colleen was training. In these quarters she met the couple's son Larry Dodge, whose towering stature recalled James Arness of television's "Gunsmoke." Dodge was then an undergraduate at Montana State University in Bozeman but the nursing student may have known him from the Bay Area. Larry Dodge was born in Oakland in 1942, the same year as Colleen.

The couple married on January 24, 1962, in Kootenai, Idaho. Daughter Tawnie came along in April of 1963, Debbie in 1966, and Wesley in May of 1969. Larry Dodge earned a PhD in sociology from Brown University, the Ivy League school in Providence, Rhode Island, and Colleen and the kids were still with him there. Colleen told friends she would do Larry's homework for him, and that she worked as a fashion model to bring in extra money. This account may constitute evidence of Colleen's tendency, noted by family and friends alike, to fabricate and embellish. Colleen dressed well and did possess a certain elegance, but nobody would mistake her for Jaclyn Smith or Cheryl Tiegs.

As Colleen told her longtime friend, Larry Dodge was unfaithful and abusive, so Colleen left him, bought a converted school bus, and drove

10

back to Montana with the kids. There she found an abandoned cabin and lived there with the children. Larry Dodge's whereabouts at this time remain unclear but he did serve as professor at the University of Montana at Missoula. Colleen divorced him in 1975, a year after she moved to Placerville, California, the "hub of the Mother Lode," as the city bills itself.

By the mid-1970s, when Jerry Brown was governor the first time, Placerville had yet to surpass a population of 10,000, give or take a few. The gold was long gone or inaccessible, and the town at the junction of highways 50 and 49 became known for lumber, wineries, and tourism. There in the Sierra foothills, Colleen would soon encounter another man.

James Roger Batten was born on October 4, 1938, in Washington State. He graduated from Fortuna High School near Eureka, in California's redwood country. Though not of great stature, he was quick and athletic enough to play basketball for the Lumberjacks of Humboldt State University. In 1957 he joined the U.S. Air Force and served at Stead Air Force Base near Reno, Nevada.

Originally Reno Army Air Base, it was used during World War II to train transport crews to fly supply routes over the Himalayas. Pilots flew out of Fairfield in the valley and over the Sierra Nevada into Stead, renamed after Croston Stead of Reno, who crashed and died on a training mission. In 1951 the base began hosting the USAF Survival School, where the Strategic Air Command (SAC) trained pilots how to survive and escape capture if shot down. Airman First Class Jim Batten was one of those instructors, and served with distinction. Stead also hosted groups of Boy Scouts, and Jim Batten was their instructor of choice.

Batten conducted survival training for a group of scouts from the Explorer Post 54, Stanford Area Council. On April 6, 1959, their leader Bob Ballou wrote to Col. Joseph H. Sherwood, Commander of the 3635th Flying Training Group. Mr. Ballou said "I would like to praise the wonderful job our group instructor did during the course. His conduct was beyond reproach." For Mr. Ballou, "Jim Batten, in my opinion, is a very good instructor and example of the best of the Air Force." In fact, "not once did he waiver from his standard," and Jim Batten "was always open to suggestions and correction."

Just before graduation from high school, Jim Batten met elegant, dark-haired Freida Stone and the two hit it off. He was not what she called a "book person," but Freida admired his intelligence and practical mind.

"He was anchored in this world, and had a great curiosity about its function," Freida recalled. "Practical arts attracted and entertained him."

Freida also liked Jim's ability to teach and adapt quickly to the student's level. They married in 1961 in Reno, Nevada, and Freida talked Jim into growing a Van Dyke beard. Nephew Terry Stone thought this made his uncle Jim look like Maynard G. Krebs, the beatnik character played by Bob Denver on "The Many Loves of Dobie Gillis." Freida thought it made him look like Peter Yarrow of Peter, Paul and Mary, who was also the same height and born the same year. Such was the resemblance that when the couple attended one of the trio's concerts, fans duly followed Jim around. He was not much of a music fan but fond of comedies such as *What's New Pussycat*, written by Woody Allen, with Peter Sellers, Peter O'Toole and Ursula Andress holding up the cast. Jim and Freida saw it several times.

After Jim finished his stint in the Air Force the couple moved back to Goldendale, Washington. There Jim worked for the soil conservation service, trained in surveying, and worked as an operating engineer on the Columbia River. The couple moved to Roseville, California, north of Sacramento when Jim found work on the Hell Hole dam and reservoir in Placer County. In 1963 he suffered a herniated disk that would trouble him for years.

In 1966 Jim and Freida moved to San Francisco where Jim worked on the tunnels for the Bay Area Rapid Transit (BART). He remained a basketball enthusiast and the couple attended games of the San Francisco Warriors. Freida, a more literary type, attended San Francisco State. The couple had no children of their own but spent much time with niece Kyleen and nephews Tamron, Christopher and Terry Stone, then living 100 miles away in Roseville. Despite his back trouble, Jim never hesitated to play baseball, croquet or badminton with the kids. Jim Batten loved to hunt and fish, but his major sport was golf, and he spent many hours playing with Freida's father Fred Stone.

Batten's Air Force survival training equipped him with vast knowledge of the Sierra and he took his nephews on camping trips at high elevations.

He showed the kids how to start a fire in wet conditions and create a bed out of boughs and moss. He could find his way by the stars, and travel by day without a compass. The kids looked up to him as a compassionate and thoughtful man, with a love of learning and teaching. Jim Batten used a crank-operated Curta mechanical calculator, very high-tech for its time, to teach the kids mathematics. Batten also schooled Terry in use of the slide-rule, then a staple of instruction.

While living in San Francisco Jim and Freida began to drift apart and before the sixties had run its course they divorced in amicable fashion. Freida went on to earn a master's degree in library science from the University of California, and later worked as a librarian in Oakland. Jim got a job in Downieville, up in Sierra County. He finished his surveying courses and began to work in that trade around the Sierra foothills. The recently divorced Colleen Dodge sought someone to survey some property, and Jim Batten answered the call.

Batten could not match Larry Dodge in stature, but Colleen found him attractive and liked the way he could make her laugh. He knew the region, loved the outdoors, and excelled at his job. Jim enjoyed Colleen's company but her past remained something of a mystery. As Jim Batten explained to ex-wife Freida, with whom he remained good friends, Colleen claimed her first husband had been involved with the Mafia, and was currently stalking her. That menacing profile did not exactly square with Larry Dodge, a sociology professor who earned his PhD at Brown University. On the other hand, Colleen's powers of persuasion were such that Jim believed her, and protecting Colleen and her children became a powerful motivating force. In effect, Jim Batten would be the family's survival trainer. He was not Catholic but his sense of empathy and respect made allowance for Colleen's convictions.

Colleen and Jim married on November 25, 1975, in Reno, Nevada. The couple worked together surveying property, and Jim duly adopted Colleen's three children, Tawnie, Deborah and Wesley. For their part, the three kids were thrilled to have him, and even called him "dad."

On a three-day visit in 1984, Jim's nephew Terry Stone found that Colleen's kids were affectionately draped all over him when he came in the door, hanging on his every word. Jim Batten helped with math homework in his typical laid-back, patient manner. Terry saw an easy, teasing banter between them and they all seemed very happy together, swimming in the pool and playing games in the yard.

As Terry departed, his uncle took him aside and said that Colleen's kids had filled "that empty space in my heart," just as Terry and his siblings had as children, and this had made him happy. As Terry saw it, "he really loved them, and it was clear to me that all he wanted to do was be a dad for real. It seemed to me his wish had finally come true and I was so glad for him." Jim's friends had similar impressions.

Michael Bowker, a journalist who covered the El Dorado County Board of Supervisors and Planning Commission for the Placerville *Mountain Democrat*, found Jim Batten upbeat and fun-loving. On Saturdays the pair played golf at the Cold Springs club northwest of town. Batten also suggested that the desk-bound Bowker also help him one day a week in his surveying business, and the journalist and photographer did so for a year. As he discovered, Jim Batten had built up a land portfolio worth $1 million, possibly more.

Bowker and his wife would dine with Colleen and Jim at the Tortilla Flats restaurant in Placerville, and sometimes at their Wilderness Way home south of town near Diamond Springs. Bowker also hit it off with the kids and accompanied them on a road trip to Pebble Beach in the family's Mercedes-Benz sedan. Batten and Bowker also took Wesley white-water rafting on the Snake River in Idaho, one of many wilderness excursions. Batten treated Wesley like a son, and wanted him to some day take over the surveying business.

To Bowker, as to Terry Stone, Jim and Colleen Batten seemed happy. She would tell stories of running off her first husband with a shotgun in Montana, laughing as she did so. That did not exactly follow her description of Larry Dodge as a Mafia gangster who was stalking her. The guests didn't take the stories seriously, considering them an attempt to make her seem a little less diminutive. And Bowker did not consider the tales a sign of trouble in her current marriage. Jim, meanwhile, had been surveying more than property.

He had shed the Van Dyke beard and the moustache was nearly all gray, but with his full head of dark hair he still struck a ruggedly handsome figure. He got involved with a woman of high social position around El Dorado County, but it still came as something of a surprise when, in June of 1985, Jim Batten told his friend he was planning to leave Colleen. He had not broken the news to her, and that raised an issue. Like the HAL 9000 computer in *2001: A Space Odyssey*, it wasn't clear how she would respond to an attempt at disconnection.

As Jim's business partner, Colleen had come to know key local players such as Fred Deberry, former chief surveyor for El Dorado County. Colleen would bring in various maps for Deberry's review, and he would order the requisite soil reports. But it wasn't all business. Deberry, his wife, and other surveyors had attended an open house at the home of Batten and his wife Colleen on Wilderness Way.

Placerville is roughly halfway between the state capital of Sacramento and Lake Tahoe. The town sits at an elevation of about 1900 feet, not high enough to avoid the blast-furnace summer heat of the valley. In July of 1985 the temperature topped out at 104, and it was already sizzling at 10 a.m. on July 27, 1985. On that Saturday, Fred Deberry met with Jim Batten in the parking lot of Beno's department store.

Deberry accompanied Batten to the Mosquito area of El Dorado County and there examined one of Batten's surveying projects for the purpose of a report on the ground conditions. Deberry duly found some corners and completed his work on the property. After lunch, about 1:30 p.m., the two men parted company in Beno's parking lot. Batten did not say what he planned to do the rest of the day.

Traffic tooled through town on Highway 50 and sunset brought some relief. Placerville is not known for nightlife but locals flowed into eateries and bars such as the Liar's Bench on Main Street, near the historic hanging spot and just a few blocks from the El Dorado County Courthouse.

That evening, sometime after eight, Mrs. Batten spoke by telephone with her father Irwin "Irish" Yates, who now lived close by at 3248 Wilderness Court in Placerville. Colleen told her father that Jim had been shot. Yates, who used to keep a shotgun in his liquor store, asked his daughter who shot him.

"I don't know," she said.

Her father seemed to know what had happened.

"There's two things you should do," Irish Yates said. "Get a hold of yourself and call the police and also call your lawyer."

That was actually three things and Colleen would do them all, but not in that order. At 8:13 p.m. Colleen Batten called her attorney, David Weiner. As it happened, Mr. Weiner had represented Jim Batten in a case involving Colleen's oldest daughter Tawnie. And now Jim had been shot. More than an hour later, at 9:22 p.m. Colleen finally called the police.

Cynthia Carroll, a public safety dispatcher for the El Dorado County Sheriff's Department, answered the phone.

"911," Carroll said.

"I need the Sheriff's office."

"You're speaking through dispatch. Can I help you?"

"Yes, is there someone I could talk to?"

"What's the problem?"

"I think I shot my husband."

A brief pause followed.

"What's the address?"

"It's 4721 Wilderness Way."

"And what does Wilderness Way run off of?"

"Uh, Pleasant Valley Rd."

"And your last name, please."

"Batten."

"And your phone number there?"

The caller rattled off the number.

"Were you having an argument when this occurred?"

"Uh, yes, I think," Mrs. Batten said. "I don't know. I don't remember anything. I don't know if I even shot him."

"Is he there in the house with you?"

"Uh, I think so."

"Standby, taking an emergency call."

"Please don't send any sirens up here," Mrs. Batten said.

"Okay," Carroll said. "Does he need an ambulance?"

"I don't think so."

Though she claimed not to remember "anything," not even whether she had shot her husband, Mrs. Batten was right about that. Her husband Jim Batten didn't need an ambulance.

"Is he dead?"

"Okay," Carroll said. "Will you stay on the phone with me?"

"Yeah. I'm not going to go anywhere."

The dispatcher could not find Wilderness Way on the map, so she asked Batten for directions.

"1200 feet past Hank's Exchange, heading east," she said. "You take a right and its, stay on the paved part of road, third house on the paved part. It's a large three-story shake house with a big 20 by 30 deck in the front and there's some lights on the outside, I think."

"How long ago did this happen?"

"I don't know," Batten said.

"You don't know?" said the startled dispatcher, who had just been given precise directions and architectural details including the dimensions of the deck. As it happened, one of the officers was familiar with the area, the dispatcher said, and would be there shortly.

"Is there anybody else in the house with you?"

"No."

"Just yourself?"

"Yes."

"All right," dispatcher Carroll said. "We'll get someone there as soon as we can. I'll tell them."

"Please."

"Thank you."

Batten hung up and the officers departed, without some key

17

information. So Carroll placed another call to Mrs. Batten, the woman who thought she had shot her husband.

"Can you tell me where the gun is?"

Carroll could not make out the response.

"Where are you in the house?"

"In the living room."

"And where is your husband, in the bedroom?"

"On the floor."

"Do you think you blacked out or did you fall asleep for a while? Do you recall what happened?"

"I think I. . ."

"You don't know?" Carroll said. "When did you have the argument that you had? Earlier today? Was it just recently?"

"It was today."

"Today?"

"He wanted me to come here today."

"Are you separated?"

"No."

"Uh-huh. Where do you live?"

"He told me he was going to shoot me if I didn't. . . He told me he was going to shoot me."

"Okay," Carroll said. "Where do you usually live?"

"I was up the hill. We were sleeping together."

"Uh-huh. Where were you when he called you and told you to come to the house?"

"I was up the hill," said Mrs. Batten. "Don't bring sirens up here, okay?"

"Okay, no sirens, I'll tell them."

Mrs. Batten signed off but another dispatcher called.

"Hi, Mrs. Batten. Hi there. This is another dispatcher. I want to keep you on the phone with me, okay? Are you okay?"

"Yes."

"Okay, all right, you say you are in the living room?"

"Yes."

"Okay. When some officers come to the door, can you see them? Can you see their headlights when they come in?"

"Huh?"

"You can? Okay. Have you got any dogs at the house or anything?"

"No."

"No, okay, what kind of car do you have out in front of the house?"

"Ah, a beige Datsun pickup."

"Okay. 10-4, 10-4. Mrs. Batten, do you know where the gun is?"

"No."

"No? You don't have it with you now?"

"No."

"You don't have it in your hand or on the table or anything?"

"No."

"Okay."

"I'll tell you when the officers get there and I want you to go out the front door and talk to them, okay?"

Mrs. Batten responded with a request of her own.

"Don't turn the sirens on, okay? Don't let them turn the sirens on."

The strange demand sparked the dispatcher's curiosity.

"Why? You don't want the neighbors to know?"

"No," she said, followed by something the dispatcher could not make out.

"Okay, all right. Get hold of yourself, you're going to be okay."

"Oh, God."

"You're going to be all right."

"He's lying on the floor."

That was not a response to a question, and it raised an issue. Mrs. Batten claimed not to remember anything but she knew for certain that her husband was on the floor. The dispatcher did not pursue the point.

"Okay. Don't worry. We're sending an ambulance, too."

"And he won't get up."

"That's all right, all right, get hold of yourself. Take a deep breath."

"He said he was going to kill me. Oh, God."

"Okay, get a hold of yourself."

"The sirens are on."

"All right, hold on. I'll be right back."

The dispatcher then addressed the officers.

19

"She didn't know where the gun is, she's in the living room, he's in the bedroom and she's not answering the phone."

Street lighting does not exactly abound in rural El Dorado County and it was pitch black by 9:34 p.m., when deputy William Crutchley arrived at 4721 Wilderness Way. There he met Mrs. Batten at the front door and asked her if she was the lady who had called in and reported that she had shot her husband.

"Is he dead?" Mrs. Batten said. She didn't know where the gun was but told Crutchley her husband was "upstairs in the bedroom." Crutchley scaled the stairs and entered the bedroom, where a television was still on. Between the bed and the window Crutchley saw a man lying on his right side. The bedspread was covered with blood spatter and on the bedspread lay a newspaper soaked with blood, a revolver, and a remote control unit for the television. Crutchley checked the body for vital signs and found none. Neither did Charles Ball, the deputy with the coroner's division, who arrived shortly thereafter. Ball did observe a large amount of blood on the floor, and that the blood was in part coagulated. By approximately 11:15, when they placed Mr. Jim Batten in the body bag, the extremities of the victim were stiff.

In the living room, Eldorado County Sheriff's deputy Dennis Theis asked Mrs. Batten what happened.

"He said he was going to kill me," she said. Theis asked if this threat was the result of an altercation.

"Yes," Mrs. Batten said.

Theis advised her of her constitutional rights, but Mrs. Batten continued to make statements over a space of 30 minutes. She spoke softly and held a pillow close to her face, but Theis, who was taping the conversation, could make out some of what she said.

"I must have shot him," Mrs. Batten told the deputy. "Did I shoot him?"

She told Theis she had built the house, and that her children were in Timber Cove, over on the coast north of San Francisco. She also said, "I don't want to talk right now."

Deputies Theis and Crutchley duly transported Mrs. Colleen Batten to the El Dorado County Jail on Forni Road. Local officials did not make it a priority to inform the victim's relatives.

Some time later, a friend of Jim and Gary Stone came across an article in the *Sacramento Bee* on the death of Jim Batten. Gary called his mother, Lessie Stone, who called Freida Batten, who could tell by Lessie's voice that something was wrong. The tragic news had been a terrible blow to the woman, who had been fond of Jim. Lessie asked if Freida had spoken to Jim recently, but she had not done so. So it came as a shock that her former husband, whose name she still used, had departed this life in sudden and violent fashion. Freida didn't know the details but duly called Jim's sister Eileen. No family member or friend would get much information from the obituary in the Placerville *Mountain Democrat*, which bills itself as California's oldest newspaper.

"James R. Batten, 48, of Placerville died July 27 in his home," the obituary said. "Mr. Batten was born in Washington and had been a resident of El Dorado County for the past 12 years. He was a self-employed surveyor. Mr. Batten was a member of the El Dorado County Land Surveyors Association and Cold Springs Golf and Country Club. He is survived by his wife, Colleen Batten of Placerville; daughters Connie Burton of Placerville and Debbie Batten of Stockton; son Wesley Batten of Placerville; mother Elizabeth Fuhrman of Washington. Private family services will be held at Memory Chapel."

Connie should have been Tonnie or Tawnie. She and Debbie were not, in fact, the victim's daughters, and Wesley was not his son. Readers would get more information about how Mr. Batten had died "in his home" in the *Mountain Democrat's* July 31, 1985, story headlined "Husband killed; wife surrenders." Colleen Ann Batten, 43, of Diamond Springs, a "slender dark-haired woman," was held on $200,000 bail in the El Dorado County Jail "on murder charges stemming from the shooting death of her 47-year-old husband James Roger Batten." The article cited Lt. Bill Wilson that the shooting appears to have grown out of a family dispute, and that Batten and his wife were living in separate residences. Colleen Batten had reportedly told police her husband had thrown her out of the house that belonged to both of them.

According to the *Mountain Democrat*, "Colleen Batten has invoked her right and is no longer talking to the detectives." Her arraignment was continued at the request of attorney Thomas Van Noord, who was "appearing for her attorney of record, David Weiner." The dapper UC

Berkeley grad Weiner, then 43, earned his JD at McGeorge School of Law in Stockton. In the Sierra foothills, Weiner was an attorney on the rise, known for taking on tough cases. The article did not reveal that on July 27, 1985, Colleen Batten called Mr. Weiner at 8:13 p.m. – more than an hour before she called the police. That was not the order her father Irish Yates had suggested.

The criminal complaint charged that Colleen Ann Batten "did willfully, unlawfully, and with malice aforethought murder James Batten, a human being, in violation of Section 187 of the California penal code, a felony." The complaint further alleged that in the commission of that offense, Colleen Ann Batten, "personally used a firearm, to wit, a shotgun, within the meaning of Penal Code Section 12022.5."

The July 31, 1985, arraignment revealed that Colleen Batten was a ten-year resident of the county, self-employed in a business, a property owner, and a person with no prior criminal record. Deputy District Attorney Walter Miller said she posed no threat to the community and the incident, "appears to be a domestic relations matter." That appraisal differed little from the statement of Colleen Batten's attorney, David Weiner.

"She has been a credit to the community and her family her entire life," said Weiner, who had not known his client her entire life. "She does have medical and physical problems that require a lot of medication right now, and it is difficult for her to get those properly in the jail, going through their procedures. There are also a number of other appointments in connection with her health that we are anxious to keep and can do much better if she is out of custody."

Weiner had brought along his client's children Tawnie, Debbie and Wesley.

"They are all outstanding people in this community," he said. "In fact, Tawnie was salutatorian last year at El Dorado High School, and she is an honor student now and just completed her first year as an engineering major at UOP." In reality, Debbie, not Tawnie, was the University of the Pacific student.

On Friday, August 2, 1985, the *Mountain Democrat* reported that, according to Weiner, Colleen had been "disoriented" when she made statements such as "I must have shot him," and "did I shoot him?"

Two days after the killing, according to the article, investigators found a single-shot shotgun on a gun rack in the closet of an office on the main floor of the Batten home, and a partial box of shotgun shells in a drawer. Evidence for the search warrant included a September 1979 Sheriff's report in which Colleen Batten "reportedly accused her husband of raping her then 16-year-old daughter." Colleen Batten "then called central dispatch reportedly saying she was going to kill her husband before threatening him with an unloaded pistol and telling him to get out of the house." Deputies "arrested and booked James Batten on suspicion of rape but charges were later dropped at Colleen's request." As David Weiner explained, "she wanted to keep her family together, to keep her family intact and to work everything out."

Colleen's bail was reduced and she agreed to the date of September 6 for the preliminary hearing, where David Weiner would again be at her side. In the meantime Colleen Batten, long-time county resident and credit to the community, according to her lawyer, was walking free. Surveyor Jim Batten, Air Force survival trainer and outdoorsman, was dead, gunned down with a firearm, to wit, a shotgun. The case marked an anniversary of sorts, with a kind of fearful symmetry.

Twenty years earlier, in 1965, "Shotgun," by Junior Walker and the All Stars, had been riding the charts, addressed to a woman. Put on your red dress, the hit tune said, and buy yourself a shotgun. You break it down, load it up, and then you shoot before he runs. That was how it all broke down on Wilderness Way on July 27, 1985. Colleen Batten got herself a shotgun, broke it down and loaded it up, then shot former survival trainer Jim Batten twice, before he could run. That is, she shot him before he could divorce her and depart. The killing also called to mind a once-common phrase.

"Shotgun wedding" normally applies to cases in which one or both parties is forced into a marriage because of an unplanned pregnancy. By deploying a shotgun to end a marriage by killing the other party, Colleen Batten duly expanded the concept. Around Placerville the hills were alive with talk of the case.

"I don't remember anything."

Placerville derives its name from the Placer gold deposits that drew thousands to the Sierra foothills during the gold rush of the late 1840s, but not all the newcomers were content to dig up the glittering stuff for themselves. Murders and robberies became commonplace and in 1848 three executions in the Dry Diggins mining camp prompted a name change to Hangtown. In 1854 it was the third-largest town in California, surpassed only by San Francisco and Sacramento. To the chagrin of the politically correct, Placerville is still known as Hangtown and remains something of a rowdy and redneck place. On the other hand, law-abiding locals no longer string up criminals from a tree.

Robberies, rapes, murders and such get adjudicated in the El Dorado County Courthouse on Main Street. Highway 50 runs right behind the stately building, which goes back to 1913, before World War I. Two Civil War cannon stand out front and portraits of bearded judges line the lobby. On September 6, 1985, this courthouse hosted the preliminary hearing in case number 31060, The People of the State of California versus Colleen Ann Batten. She showed up in a ruffled pink blouse and burgundy skirt, a style and color scheme she would favor throughout the proceedings.

The District Attorney at the time was Ronald Tepper, a UCLA law grad who had moved to Placerville in 1974 to become chief deputy to judge Terrence Finney and became DA in 1977. According to a reporter who covered the court, Tepper was known to be tough on crime and would have been the best man to handle the case. But Tepper would hand it off to Deputy District Attorney Walter Miller, a local man with a reputation as a nice guy, not necessarily an asset in a murder trial.

After Batten's death, the district attorney had talked to the victim's friend Michael Bowker for several hours, and the journalist heard Colleen's account on the 911 tape. Miller told Bowker Colleen had reloaded the weapon and shot Jim Batten again. Despite these realities, Colleen's three children insisted their mother was innocent and wanted Bowker to join them in support of Colleen. Bowker told them he could not do that, which the kids took hard.

Miller told Judge Lloyd B. Hamilton he was going to call Debbie Batten, Colleen's daughter, and that her son Wes Batten "may be a witness." That day Wes did not appear and the people called Dr. Robert Anthony, M.D. a forensic pathologist who had trained at Case Western in Cleveland, Ohio, and Duke University in Durham, North Carolina. Of the 600 autopsies the doctor had performed, some 60 involved gunshot victims.

Miller asked Dr. Anthony if, on July 29 of that year, he had performed an autopsy on a person by the name of James Batten.

"I did," Anthony said.

"Objection," said defense attorney David Weiner. "This is hearsay."

The objection startled the courtroom, but there was precedent for it. In similar style, Irving Kanarek, defense attorney in the trial of Charles Manson, had objected to a witness stating his name on the grounds that he heard it from his mother. The name was not hearsay and neither was the autopsy question at hand.

As in the 1967 movie *In the Heat of the Night*, they had the body, which was dead. Photographs and other evidence established that the subject of the autopsy was James Roger Batten, "a well developed, well nourished adult, white male who had suffered two gunshot injuries to his chest," according to Dr. Anthony. David Weiner's theatrical objection suggested that, though deceased, Mr. Batten somehow posed a threat to the attorney's case.

Dr. Anthony had spent three to four hours on the autopsy and concluded, "Mr. Batten died as a result of multiple gunshot wounds." As Anthony described it, wound number one was 16 inches down from top of the head, two and a half inches from the right of the midline of the body. It was almost circular, one and three quarter inches by one and a half inches. And Anthony found multiple injuries around the edge of the wound caused by shotgun pellets, an example of "satelloid injuries."

The shot entered between third and fourth ribs and proceeded downward at a steep angle causing "a large amount of damage" to the right lung and injuries to the diaphragm and liver. The pathologist also found circular pieces of cardboard which "appeared to be wadding from a shotgun shell." The wound also caused minor damage to upper portion of the heart the right atrial appendage. Dr. Anthony found a large amount of blood present in the chest on the right-hand side.

"There was no exit" for the wound, he testified. "The wound tract ended in the liver." The angle of the wound was "almost vertical," maybe ten degrees off. The first wound was a "rather serious injury," a "lethal injury" that "could cause death over a matter of minutes to a longer period."

The second shotgun injury was in the left lateral chest, 19 inches from top of head and 10 inches to the left of midline. It was elliptical in shape and one and a quarter inches long by three quarter inches wide. The edges were ragged and irregular, with a small amount of satelliting but no powder residue.

The second wound entered between fourth and fifth ribs and caused "massive injury to left lung, and injury to arch of the aorta, the major artery off of the heart." Dr. Anthony found a "large number of shotgun pellets in the lung, in the bloody fluid in the left part of the chest." In the plural space he found "two pieces of felt wadding." This wound was on a horizontal plane, going slightly backwards, and there was no exit wound.

With the "massive injury to the top of the heart," Dr. Anthony said, the second wound "would result in death within a matter of moments."

The lethality of both shots confirmed that the shooter had taken careful aim. The absence of defensive wounds on the hands and arms suggested the victim had been taken by surprise. The recovered pellets and wadding were consistent with a .410 shotgun.

"Objection, unless there's some foundation for that," David Weiner said. "Move to strike."

Judge Hamilton asked Anthony the basis of his opinion.

The size of the wadding, Anthony said, "accurately reflects the size of the bore of the shotgun, a small bore .410. Wadding from 20, 16 and 12-gauge shotguns is "much larger than what we recovered from the body of Mr. Batten."

Weiner maintained his objection but Miller said he would submit the testimony. The judge asked Anthony how many of his autopsies involved shotgun wounds. That turned out to be two or three dozen, and with varying sizes of shotguns. So Hamilton overruled the objection.

A .410 shotgun is an entry-level long gun normally used for small game, pests and such. This firearm happens to be the least powerful shotgun, but as Dr. Anthony's testimony had confirmed, nobody wants to be standing in front of one when it goes off. True to form, Mr. Batten had a "large amount of blood" on his arms and had been dead four to six hours before the first photos. That timing also drew an objection from Weiner.

The wound in the right upper chest, Anthony testified, occurred first because there was a "large amount of hemorrhage" with that injury and "almost none" with the other. If number two had been first, "the massive degree of injury would have put blood pressure close to zero and probably the heart would have stopped. The person in this state is not capable of bleeding forcefully or profusely."

In his cross-examination, Weiner asked Anthony when he first saw the body. That turned out to be 10 a.m. on July 29.

"Did you ever inspect a 12-gauge shotgun."

"Yes."

"Have you inspected a 16-gauge shotgun?"

"Yes."

"And a .410 shotgun?"

"I have."

"And a 10-gauge?"

"On one occasion."

"Have you inspected shells that can be fired in each of those gauged weapons?"

"I have."

"Have you compared the size of the waddings in each of those gauges?"

"I have."

"When did you do that?"

"I did that as part of my training in advanced forensic pathology at the Armed Forces Institute of Pathology."

That Institute is as good as it gets, which is why countless civilian pathologists train there. As they know from experience, lethal gunshot wounds are not limited to military combat.

The waddings in Mr. Batten, proceedings revealed, had been soaked in blood and had not expanded very much, no more than 10 to 15 percent.

Weiner asked about other weapons beside the .410 that fire shotgun type cartridges. Was the doctor familiar with handguns that can fire shotgun shells?

"I am familiar with pistols that use a form of snake shot, similar to shotgun pellets," Anthony said, "but it is not a shotgun cartridge." Such cartridges had no wadding and Anthony had never seen a handgun that fires actual shotgun shells. The Civil War vintage LeMat revolver does so, but the weapon is exceedingly rare. Modern pistols that fire actual shotgun shells did not appear until decades later.

In further testimony, Anthony acknowledged that the body could have been lying on its back or bent over forward when the shot entered. But there were "numerous" other possibilities. In discussion of the wounds, Anthony said the weapon had been fired from a distance of "two feet or greater" and the second wound "would cause death as close to instantaneous as you can."

The distance was a significant detail. As an Air Force survival trainer Batten had to be keenly aware of what was going on around him at all times. That an assailant wielding a loaded shotgun had got so close was evidence that the victim had been at rest and taken by surprise. Batten's quick reflexes would have given him a fighting chance to disarm the assailant or at least deflect the weapon. He had no chance because he did not see the shots coming. Lying in wait is a common enhancement in murder cases but Miller did not pursue it at the time.

He then called Fred Deberry, the civil engineer and land surveyor familiar with James Batten. Deberry testified that he saw James Batten on July 27 about 10 in morning. "We went out and looked at one of his survey projects, and I left my car at Beno's parking lot up in the other part of town."

Deberry last saw James Batten about 1:30 that day, in Beno's parking lot.

"Did he make any comment concerning what he was going to do the rest of the day?" Miller said.

"No, he didn't," and Deberry said he did not inquire.

"And directing your attention to the young lady sitting next to Mr. Weiner in court," Miller said. "Do you recognize that person?"

"Yes," the witness said.

"By what name?"

"By Mrs. Batten. Colleen."

Miller asked if he knew her. Deberry told the court he handled projects for Colleen and her husband as county surveyor, and after that time. And he had been to the Batten home one time for a social event.

Miller asked whom Deberry meant by her husband. Was that James Batten?

"Yes," said Deberry, who was then excused.

Criminalist Michael Saggs of the California Department of Justice had run some tests and concluded that the second shot had been fired from "between two and four feet" from the victim.

The weapon was a single-shot, top-break shotgun, with a 26-inch barrel. Saggs outlined how it had to be reloaded for every shot. He also identified a single-action six-shot revolver. If only one bullet was in that gun, Saggs testified, to be fired it would have to be in the chamber one away from the hammer.

Police had recovered a box of Winchester Super Speed shotgun shells. All had number 9 shot except one round, a slug. That was an Imperial, a Canadian shell. All the others were Winchesters.

Witness Lynn Wheaton worked as a public safety dispatcher for the El Dorado County Sheriff's department. She had brought a tape from July 27,1985, taken at 9:22 and 50 seconds in the evening.

Colleen Batten, decked out in pink and burgundy, had been calm and relaxed as she listening to testimony. Then they started the tape.

"I think I shot my husband," she heard her own voice say.

"When she heard her voice in the courtroom," wrote Claire Wood of the *Mountain Democrat*, "she appeared more agitated, leaning forward and putting her hands to her face."

The dispatcher asked if this had been in the course of an argument.

"Uh, yes, I think," the tape said. "I don't know. I don't remember anything. I don't know if I even shot him."

Asked if he needed an ambulance, she said, "I don't think so." But she didn't know when the shooting had happened.

The court also played back the section when dispatcher Cynthia Carroll called back.

"Can you tell me where the gun is?"

Colleen Batten's response to that question was inaudible, but the court heard her say: "He told me he was going to shoot me if I didn't. . . He told me he was going to shoot me."

Deputy William Crutchley, for five years a patrol officer with the Eldorado County Sheriff's office, next took the stand, telling the court he had three and a half years experience investigating deceased persons and handled 98 percent of the coroner's cases in El Dorado County.

On July 27, he arrived at the Wilderness Way residence at 9:34 p.m. and met Mrs. Batten at the front door. The officer duly pointed her out in the courtroom beside her attorney David Weiner.

"I asked Mrs. Batten if she was the lady that had called in and reported that she had shot her husband," Crutchley said. Miller asked what response Mrs. Batten gave.

"Is he dead?" she had said. She didn't know where the gun was but her husband was "upstairs in the bedroom."

"What did you observe?"

"I saw the victim lying on his right side, between the bed and the window. And I saw a .22 Ruger revolver lying on the bed" near the remote control unit for the television, which was on. Deputy Crutchley did not say what program was playing at the time. He found that the victim showed no vital signs and observed blood spatter on the bedspread.

In questioning from Mr. Weiner, Crutchley said the revolver had recently been fired and that he found bloodstains in more than just one spot. Accompanying Crutchley on that call was the next witness, eight-year Eldorado County Sheriff's deputy Dennis Theis.

"I observed a female in the living room of the residence, near the front door, inside," said Theis, who pointed out Mrs. Batten. On the night of July 27, he had asked her what happened.

"He said he was going to kill me," she said, and Theis asked if this was the result of an altercation.

"Yes," Mrs. Batten said.

After Theis advised her of her constitutional rights, she made a number of statements over a space of 30 minutes. These emerged under cross-examination from David Weiner.

"I don't want to talk right now," she said. She told Theis she had built the house, and that her children were in Timber Cove.

"All you can hear on the tape recording is mainly me," Theis explained, "because she spoke in a low volume."

The officer did not say the low volume had been intentional, but some in the court might have wondered. On redirect, Mr. Miller asked Theis what Mrs. Batten said first. Theis testified that she had said:

"I must have shot him. Did I shoot him?"

That brought objections from Weiner, who objected to the deputy reading from his report. Theis later said "most of the time she was talking as she was seated. She had a pillow on her lap that she was hugging, holding the pillow to her mouth, holding her hands over her mouth when she spoke."

"Was she crying?" Weiner asked.

"At times, yes."

"Was she distraught?"

"I believe so," Theis said but "not hysterical."

"Emotionally drawn?"

"I wouldn't describe it like that," Theis said. "I would describe it as acting like she was in a type of mental stupor of sorts."

Colleen Batten also told Theis that Jim Batten called her daughter from an earlier marriage a "contentious bitch," and had raped the girl since she was 12. The *Mountain Democrat* took notice of that in a September 9, 1985, article by Claire Wood headlined, "Daughter agrees slain stepfather 'unpredictable.'"

During testimony, meanwhile, Weiner asked Theis, "She never told you she killed her husband, did she?"

"No."

"She never told you she shot him either, did she?"

"No, not in those words."

"She didn't tell you that, 'I shot my husband,' did she?"

"No."

Weiner had no further questions.

Theis gave way to Charles Ball a deputy with the Sheriff's coroner division. He too had been on the scene and Miller asked for his observations "concerning what appears to be blood close to the body on the floor."

"Yes," Ball said. "There was a large quantity or a heavy quantity of blood. It was a very deep red color and it was coagulated in parts. It was a large amount of blood."

When they placed James Batten in a body bag, his extremities were "stiff, in a stiffened position" and at that time it was approximately 11:15-11:20 p.m.

Sgt. William Wilson, El Dorado County detective, told the court he had retrieved the weapons, finding one live round in the revolver, right under the loading gate, but no spent cartridges. Likewise, Wilson found lead pellets scattered across the bed, but no spent shotgun shells or cartridges. The detective recovered a .410 shotgun not in the bedroom but in an office area on the middle floor, "in a closet hanging on a rack." Wilson could not tell whether it had recently been fired and found the weapon unloaded.

In cross examination with Mr. Weiner, Wilson said Colleen Batten's fingerprints had not been found on the gun. Blood work had not yet been performed on the bedspread.

Later in the session, when admitting evidence, Weiner said "I would move to strike Dr. Anthony's testimony. I don't believe that the foundation that was stated to the court to be shown was shown."

For those in the courtroom, Mr. Weiner's motion to strike was both audacious and revealing. The attorney had not presented evidence contradicting Dr. Anthony's finding that Jim Batten had been shot twice with a shotgun, and that the second wound entered between fourth and fifth ribs and inflicted a massive injury to the heart, causing death in a matter of moments. By moving to strike, Mr. Weiner signaled that he did not want observers of the record to consider the information Dr. Anthony presented on its merits. The attorney preferred that they not engage it at all.

"I recall the testimony," said Judge Hamilton, who overruled the objection to strike.

Walter Miller then called Debbie Batten, not yet 20 years old, who told the court she was adopted by James Batten "a year and a half ago."

She was now a student at University of the Pacific in Stockton.

Miller directed the witness to the weekend of July 27. "That's the weekend your father was shot, okay?"

"Uh-huh."

Debbie Batten further testified that on Saturday, July 27, the day of the crime, she called her mother at about 12:30. At that time, Jim Batten would still have been with Fred Deberry, according to his sworn testimony.

"To whom did you speak?"

"My sister Tawnie," she said. "No, my mom. Excuse me."

"Did you speak to both of them?"

"No, I just spoke to my mom," she said. "I was confused." But the day after she called her mother, Debbie Batten did see Tawnie, which she also spelled Tonnie.

"We ran out of gas in Davis, and I called home to tell my mom and see if she could help us out, and my sister answered the phone."

Asked what time she made the call, Debbie said "I think it was around 3:00. I don't know." But an hour later, she saw Tawnie.

"When was the last time you had any communication with your father?"

"It would be Tuesday, the week before."

"Sometime you received some information that your father had been killed, is that right?"

"Well, yes."

"When did you receive that information, initially, the first time?"

"My sister told me when she came and picked us up in Davis."

Under questioning from Weiner, Debbie says she saw Jim Batten the Tuesday before the kids went on the camping trip in Timber Cove.

"He took me out shopping that day."

"How long did you spend with him?"

"About six hours," Debbie said, and he was "very nice to me that day." That is, until near the end, "and then it was like he was really mad at me." And he was "mad that I was going to talk with my mom and stuff." On the drive back, "he got really glum and down and didn't really want to talk or anything. And then we met my mom. We were at Diamond Springs Omelet House and my mom stopped in and he just flipped-flopped, totally."

That ended the questions but they weren't done. Judge Hamilton set the next date for Friday, September 13. That day Walter Miller requested that the defendant be held to answer.

"I would submit it too," said David Weiner, who cited "a situation with someone who is very distraught, who has found her husband dead, and who is making a number of comments, and none of which is to the effect that 'I killed my husband' or that 'I shot my husband.'"

"Your honor," Miller countered, "I think there is evidence before the court to associate the defendant with the killing of her husband."

Miller cited statements from the 911 transcript, "I think I shot my husband" and "Yes, I think. I don't know. I don't remember anything. I don't know if I even shot him." And Miller said, "She associates the use of the weapon to herself" and "concerning her being distraught, throughout the dispatch tape she sounds coherent. Although her voice is low she gives explicit directions an explicit description of her house to the dispatch person. So she's mentally alert, your honor, and definitely not distraught to the degree that Mr. Weiner would ask the court to believe."

When asked if her husband was in the bedroom, Mrs. Batten had responded "on the floor." Miller also cited her statements to Dennis Theis, such as "I must have shot him. Did I shoot him?" Miller told the court that the victim had been "shot twice, and the opinion is it was a .410 shotgun."

Weiner protested that no .410 shells were located on July 27 and "they didn't find a .410 shotgun either." That had happened later, he said. And he implied that the shotgun they found was not the murder weapon.

"I know of a way that two .410 shotgun shells could be fired and not be ejected," Weiner said. "It's called a double-barrel .410 shotgun." So the attorney was suggesting that the police might not have the right weapon. Several firearms companies manufacture double-barreled .410 shotguns.

When being questioned by police, Mrs. Batten was "a very distraught, emotionally drawn woman," said Weiner. "This lady was not a normal person at the time." That seemed to concede that she had indeed been the shooter.

Judge Hamilton said the court had reviewed the transcript and the evidence.

"There is a mystery of what happened during a certain period of time preceding the call to the Sheriff's office," he said. "We may never know what happened during that period of time. I think the evidence is clear that, for purposes of this hearing, that the deceased was dead for some period of time prior to the call being made." The court did not have a "full picture" but Hamilton said the defendant should be held to answer. "The defendant personally used a weapon, to wit, a shotgun, within the meaning of Penal Code Section 12022.5."

Any sense of mystery surrounding the case, meanwhile, did not include the fate of James Roger Batten, 47. On the night of July 27, 1985, Jim Batten took two blasts from a .410 shotgun, both carefully aimed from point-blank range, both lethal, and the second, as Dr. Anthony testified, causing "death as close to instantaneous as you can." Despite Weiner's objection to Anthony's testimony, none of that was in dispute.

Colleen immediately had Jim's body cremated, so Jim's friend Michael Bowker did not get a chance to say goodbye. Neither did his first wife Freida, nor her brother Gary and mother Lessie. Neither did Jim's niece Diane, or Kyleen, Tamron, Christopher and Terry Stone, who had spent many happy hours in his company.

Colleen buried Jim Batten's ashes on the Wilderness Way property, mounting a memorial plaque proclaiming that they loved him and missed him. It was an odd tribute for a man accused of raping a 12-year-old. Likewise, all three children initially kept the Batten surname. Colleen Ann Batten, the property owner and credit to her community, who had no criminal record, remained free on bail while awaiting the trial.

The judge in the case would be Charles Fogerty, who in April of 1985 had made national news in the case of Loki, a 225-lb. English Mastiff who had bitten two children, mauling one seriously. Animal control officials ordered Loki destroyed and Judge Fogerty upheld the death penalty. Loki's owner Gene Stump appealed to the California Supreme Court and Loki's life was duly spared.

Fogerty might not have been Weiner's choice, but the trial would not start until the following year, 1986. That left ample time for the defendant and her attorney, by many accounts the best in town, to plot a strategy. Trends of the time were on their side.

The feminist movement was on the march, but it wasn't all about the accomplishments of women and equal pay for equal work. As militants had it, men were a wild species of violent abusers, and women were their innocent victims. By the early 1980s lawyers began deploying "battered woman syndrome" as a defense in cases of women killing their husbands. That was exactly what Colleen Batten had done. She may not have put on a red dress and gone downtown, but she got herself a shotgun, broke it down, loaded it up, and shot Jim Batten twice before he could run.

Another part of the strategy would emerge in Colleen's telephone call to Freida Batten during preparations for the trial. Freida was not eager to speak with the woman accused of murdering her ex-husband, but the call left her curious.

"What happened?" asked Freida.

"I just don't know," Colleen said, in what Freida described as a hushed little-girl voice. "Everything turned black. I don't remember a thing." So as in the 911 call, memory problems would be an issue.

Colleen asked Freida if she would speak with her attorney David Weiner, who wanted Jim Batten's ex-wife to testify on Colleen's behalf. According to the attorney, Jim had supposedly told Colleen that Freida once tried to shoot him. It was the first Freida had heard of such a thing, and it was not true. Their divorce had been amicable and they remained good friends. Weiner also brought family court records charging Jim Batten with sexual abuse, for which he had submitted to counseling. Freida Batten told the attorney she knew nothing of that, and she had good reason to remain skeptical.

In all the 14 years she knew Jim Batten, Freida found "not a whisper of abuse, never." In her experience, Jim Batten loved kids. In similar style, Freida's brother Gary said the portrait emerging from the defendant and her lawyer was "not the Jim Batten I knew." Nephew Terry Stone, then living in Birmingham, Alabama, found the allegations a complete surprise, and didn't believe any of it.

Freida Batten told David Weiner she had nothing to contribute and would not be testifying for the defense. She never heard from Weiner or his client again. The El Dorado County district attorney never called her to testify.

National media and the *Sacramento Bee*, the major daily in the area, for the most part ignored the trial, but it was certified front-page news in Placerville, where Colleen Batten emerged as the possible victim.

"I'll let her tell the story."

"Colleen Batten – Murderess or Martyr?" ran the headline of the *Mountain Democrat* on Friday, January 31, 1986. The front-page story by Pat Lakey began:

"Although she is accused of shooting her husband in the chest with a shotgun, then ejecting the fired shell, loading another shotgun shell into the chamber and shooting him a second time through the heart, Colleen Batten sat calmly through the first four days of her trial."

Weiner's strategy became evident on the trial's second day, during voir dire, when he questioned jurors about their attitude toward "child molesters" and the subject of "oral copulation." The attorney would essentially vilify Jim Batten as a monster and portray Colleen and her children as his victims. Accusations of this type carry an implicit presumption of guilt and pack such a powerful taint that even those in the know about Jim Batten were hoping not to be called as witnesses. That included friends of Batten who worked in the El Dorado County courthouse and the upscale woman with whom he had an affair.

Walter Miller said Weiner's questions were "red herrings" to plant in the jury's mind facts not in evidence about the dead man. Jim Batten was not on trial, and could not respond, but in the early days of the trial, some key information did emerge on a different front. Jim Batten died without a will. Therefore the surviving spouse, Colleen, gets all the jointly owned property. That raised the question of motive. Miller told the court he would prove that Colleen killed in order to gain all the couple's property.

Testimony began in earnest on the trial's third day, January 29, and witnesses included William Wilson, Michael Saggs, already on record

37

about the particulars of the crime scene, and Sacramento County detective Robert Bell, an expert in bloodstain pattern analysis.

"The petite brunette sat demurely," Pat Lakey wrote in the *Mountain Democrat*, "as experts testified that the first shot destroyed part of Jim Batten's lungs and the second destroyed his heart."

This recalled testimony from the preliminary hearing that both shots had no exit wound and both shots were lethal. The second shot's "massive injury to the top of the heart," Dr. Anthony had testified, "would result in death within a matter of moments." And the recovered pellets and wadding were consistent with a .410 shotgun.

The first wound he sustained was likely fatal, testimony revealed, and the victim had no chance of surviving the second shot. Robert Bell testified that Batten had been shot the first time as he leaned over the bed. This supported testimony of pathologist who said the first shot entered the chest at a steep upward angle.

Colleen Batten's attorney had a different take on it.

"Weiner has tried to show that Batten may have been holding the gun, even trying to shoot Colleen, when he was killed," Lakey wrote. So as the attorney had it, some kind of struggle was going on.

Detective Bell had countered that the gun had no blood on it, as it would have if held in a shooting position by the victim. But no blood and no prints had been found on the weapon.

"I told her to go down to the house and see if Jim's alive or dead and call me back," Colleen's father Irwin Yates testified. He told her to call the police, but it also emerged in court that she first called David Weiner.

Fred Deberry and Eldon McComb also rendered testimony about Jim Batten, a likable man in their view. Lynn Wheaton provided the reel-to-reel tape and the jury got copies of the transcript. The jury heard Colleen Batten on the dispatch tape say "I think I shot my husband" and as Lakey wrote, the defendant "wiped away tears as the tape played."

Deputy Dennis Theis told the court what had happened when he showed up on Wilderness Way on July 27, 1985. But as Pat Lakey wrote, "the defendant never absolutely admits that she pulled the trigger of the small-bore shotgun that was used to slay James Roger Batten."

The next day William Crutchley added his account and the jury heard testimony from Colleen's daughter Tawnie Reed, now in her early 20s, towering over the petite, pink-clad brunette beside David Weiner. Tawnie testified that her stepfather Jim Batten had abused her sexually since she was 13. The abuse, she said, included forcible rape and continued up to age of 21.

Deputy District Attorney Miller played a tape in which Tawnie said her father "hadn't touched me" since the family reconciled five years ago. But on the stand Tawnie said she lied to the investigator during that phone call. The court did not learn that Jim Batten's attorney in the matter was none other than David Weiner, now representing Colleen Batten, charged with his murder.

"Weiner managed to show the jury that Colleen Batten is an accomplished woman," the *Mountain Democrat* noted. Wesley Batten, 16, told the court his mother "was down there working trying to get money for us. She kept both houses up, vacuumed, mowed lawns, did laundry" in addition to plumbing, carpentry, electrical work, and even cutting firewood. In all this "James Batten did not help her," and spent his time playing golf.

Jim Lawson of nearby Rocklin testified that he knew Jim Batten for 23 years and recalled three cases of him engaging in bar fights. The first had been in 1963 when Batten and others were camped near Sloughhouse, southeast of Sacramento, completing a surveying job. Lawson testified that during a card game inside a tent, one of the players grabbed a beer from Batten's six-pack.

"Jim got mad and jumped up and hit him," Lawson said. Two others pulled Batten off him and "he cursed the man and said leave his beer alone or he'd bust his face."

In 1972, according to Lawson, Batten pulled a phone off a receiver and said, "I guess I showed her."

In the third incident, also in a bar, "One guy kept talking while Jim was shooting. He got mad, went over and hit the guy with the pool cue." Lawson said the blow was to the neck and that Batten threw billiard balls at him, hitting him twice before he made it out the door. Daniel Russell, a golf pro at the Cold Springs Country Club, said he saw Batten lose his temper and challenge him to a fight.

According to witness Jake Raper, a county planner, Batten "became angry fairly rapidly. His face became flushed, he raised his voice and said

'If you don't lighten up, Raper, you'll get yours." Batten had supposedly tried to get Raper fired over an error on a map. Contractor Andrew Peszynski also testified about Jim Batten. It was as though the deceased man was standing trial for disorderly conduct, battery, and disturbing the peace.

Journalist Michael Bowker knew Batten better than any of those men, but Walter Miller never called him to testify and he is also missing from newspaper accounts. Bowker never saw Batten lose his temper, raise his voice or brag about fighting. In Bowker's experience, he was easy going 100 percent of the time, even when throwing down some drinks.

"Overall, I think portraying Jim as a rough bar-fighter is ridiculous," Bowker said. "He was tough, like any man, but he wasn't belligerent, at least I never saw him cause any trouble for anybody."

Had she been called, Freida Batten could have presented the April 6, 1959 letter to Col. Joseph H. Sherwood, citing Jim Batten's conduct as "beyond reproach" and calling him "the best of the Air Force." Freida Batten never got the opportunity to present the document, or profile her former husband in any way. Reporters did not contact her and no quotes from Freida Batten appear in the *Mountain Democrat* stories on the trial.

Also missing from the news stories, and the witness list, was Jim Batten's nephew Terry Stone, who recalls that no one from the DA's office ever reached out to his family. By the time of his visit to the Batten family in 1984, Stone was a juvenile officer and tuned in to subtle hints of trouble. He found none, and "nothing about Colleen struck me as particularly odd or different—certainly not dangerous." In fact, Stone said, "she seemed like a lovely woman, graceful, elegant, and welcoming." Now Colleen Batten was charged with murder and unlike Stone's uncle Jim, able to testify on her own behalf.

"I'll let her tell the story," David Weiner told Pat Lakey. She in turn asked the dapper attorney if he would try to convince the jury that Jim Batten was attempting to shoot Colleen with the handgun.

"I'll let Colleen tell about that too," he said.

But as the *Mountain Democrat* noted, she would face some problems. The Wednesday February 5 story by Pat Lakey came headlined, "Murder defendant has amnesia, expert says." Even so, on many points her memory was clear and detailed.

"Her face drawn and white, Colleen Batten described her husband of 10 years as a 'Jekyll and Hyde' personality capable of extreme violence." She testified, "He was real sweet one minute then the next he would be in a deep rage, yelling, screaming, throwing things across the room." Said the defendant, "I thought he was a very, very sick man."

She decided to get a divorce because he "was becoming more and more mean with the children, especially Wesley."

As Michael Bowker recalls, Jim Batten treated Wesley like a son, taking him on numerous white-water rafting and wilderness expeditions. But the jury never heard testimony to that effect. And it had been Jim Batten who took out divorce papers the day before Colleen shot him. But as the defendant had it, Jim Batten called her, she arrived at the house, walked upstairs and confronted him with the documents as he stood there looking out the window.

"I told him we can't go on living like this and gave him the papers," she said. "He stood there and read them then walked out." After a time, her husband returned.

"I was very upset, I didn't want to divorce him," she said. "He came in the bedroom and he was an absolute madman." His fists were clenched. There would be no divorce, and he said, "I'm going to kill you."

Colleen told the court she tried to reason with him, telling him again that he needed psychological help. But Jim said he was going to get everything the couple owned. Then he grabbed her by the hair.

"He threw me on the bed and put his knee in my stomach. I was really scared. He said he was going to kill me. He grabbed a pistol. He put it to my head and said he was going to kill me."

She said "Jim, please, I love you. I will do anything for you. You're sick and you need help so bad."

As she testified, he then told her that she was a "fool" because she was unaware that he was having sex with Colleen's daughter. "That made me feel like a stray dog," she testified. "He couldn't leave me and do that." But in her account, Jim Batten told her that her daughter "loved" oral copulation and that he was going to make Colleen do the same thing. As he forced her to complete the sex act, he still held the gun to her head.

"I heard a click and thought I was going to die," she told the court. The next thing she remembers is a phone ringing. At that time, she realized she was no longer in the house where the alleged assault occurred, but she was at the other, uphill house.

The caller was her father "He was yelling at me, wanting to know if Jim was all right or not."

Telephone records confirmed that a phone call was placed to her father from the house where the killing occurred. Colleen Batten did not remember making the call, did not remember phoning her attorney's residence, and did not remember calling 911, despite earlier testimony that she did all that. And "what she said she can't recall," as Pat Lakey's story explained, "is how James Batten suffered two shotgun wounds that killed him."

To explain why she couldn't recall the shotgun wounds that killed Jim Batten, the defense brought in Dr. Norman Tresser, who earned his medical degree at Ohio State University and trained in psychiatry at Hawaii State Hospital and Mount Zion Medical Center at the University of California in San Francisco. Dr. Tresser testified that Colleen suffered from "psychogenic amnesia," a condition that, according to the doctor, basically shuts down the memory system of the brain in self-defense.

Tresser testified that because killing someone would be so out of character for Colleen, her mind refused to remember the details. "If an incident was so overwhelming," Tresser said, "and out of keeping with a person's beliefs and morals, and the mind can't deal with it, it will shut it out. If you don't you will go crazy."

Asked whether that hypothetical situation applies to Colleen Batten, Tresser replied, "She fits."

Dr. Tresser told the court the defendant was "under chronic stress, working long hours, only sleeping three hours a night." The molestation issue was "an overwhelming threat to her mind" and when the alleged physical assault began, "the portion of the brain that automatically defends the body took over." This portion "supersedes the use of other parts of the brain, including the part that stores the memory."

As Dr. Tresser saw it, Colleen Batten was "a moral hard-working Christian mother, a good mother and wife," but within a matter of minutes she faced the prospect of total failure, so "her mind would have to protect her from that."

The reality that James Batten had been shot twice bothered Tresser not at all. The number of shots fired, he said, would not alter the state of mind.

"Did you make any tests as to whether this is a feigned amnesia?" Miller asked.

"That's difficult to do," Tresser said. In the past drugs and hypnosis had been used to induce memory. They were used now, he said, because of possible harmful effects to the person and because the tests were not reliable.

The prosecution did not tap an expert to examine Colleen Batten, perhaps to probe how her memory remained crystal clear on some facts, as with her directions to dispatcher Cynthia Carroll, but conveniently disappeared on others. Miller noted that Colleen Batten's accounts were all based on her alone, and they didn't change Miller's view that Colleen shot Jim Batten twice with the shotgun.

"Colleen Batten, murderess or martyr?" the *Mountain Democrat* wondered at the outset of the trial. On Friday, February 7, the newspaper's front-page headline posed a different question: "Batten killing justifiable homicide or murder?" As staff writer Pat Lakey framed it, "the jury must decide whether James Batten was *an unspeakably cruel man who deserved to die* or whether he was the victim of a murder by his wife after Colleen Batten learned he wanted a divorce." (emphasis added)

Even readers unschooled in the law may have detected some problems with that statement. The El Dorado County jury had not been tasked to decide whether Jim Batten was an "unspeakably cruel man," nor whether he "deserved to die." The jury had been tasked to decide whether Colleen Batten was guilty of murdering her husband James Batten, who was not on trial. And on the day of closing arguments, the prosecutor decried the "character assassination" of the deceased.

"The prosecution's chief witness is missing," Miller told the court. "He's dead. But there is a lot said by James Batten" in evidence from the body.

Police had found a blood-spattered newspaper on the bed, and Mr. Batten was probably reading it when shot, not engaging in any kind of a brutal attack. After the first shot, Jim Batten was in a defenseless position, clutching the first wound. Then Colleen administered the "coup de grace" by moving to within four feet of the victim and shooting him in the side. So even if the alleged sexual assault occurred, Miller said, her action would not be self-defense.

The handgun on the bed, Miller said, was "a plant" by Colleen Batten, who had "control of the crime scene" for at least an hour. She had "coldly and calculatedly set it up," and that was why police found no shotgun shells in the room. As for Colleen's claim of amnesia, Miller said that was too convenient to be believed.

David Weiner recalled Dr. Tresser's testimony about the psychogenic amnesia the attorney said afflicted his client. Jim Batten had not been reading a newspaper, Weiner argued, but had armed himself with a handgun and after the first shot he continued his attack. Therefore Colleen had acted in self-defense.

"You must decide whether she is a convicted murderer or a victim," Weiner told the jury. "If you make a mistake, the consequences are dire. It would be a horrible mistake to find her guilty of murder. Acquit her. Let her go home to her family. Hopefully in time the scars will heal and she'll get on with her life."

Walter Miller told the nine women and three men on jury to "consider the case without sympathy or pity, prejudice or bias. I know deciding is tough for you. Looking at Colleen Batten, she appears pleasant as dressed up. Her children here in court are well mannered. But all that is not evidence in this case. If you acquit Colleen Batten, it would be a dire consequence to the system because she murdered Jim Batten."

Miller also asked that the jury instructions include a manslaughter charge. Weiner protested it was unfair to introduce that possibility so late in the proceedings. Miller countered that the judge had full authority to do that, and even to admit new evidence, citing a Los Angeles case as precedent. Even so, Judge Fogerty denied Miller's request, so the jury would either convict Colleen Ann Batten for murder or acquit the slender dark-haired woman who had sat calmly as experts described the shotgun blasts that killed Jim Batten.

The El Dorado County jury deliberated for a day and a half. On the eighth day of the trial, February 6, 1986, the jury found Colleen Ann Batten not guilty of the crime of murder in the first degree. The jury also found the defendant not guilty of murder in the second degree. Second-degree murder is intentional but not premeditated or planned, or committed in the heat of passion. It can be a killing caused by dangerous conduct and disregard for human life. But whatever the definition, Colleen Ann Batten was not guilty of it, according to the El Dorado County jury. With a manslaughter charge not allowed, as court papers say, the "defendant is discharged."

Acquitted, in other words, an astonishing decision given the evidence. The defendant had been presumed innocent and praised for her character. Her victim, a dead man, had been presumed guilty and vilified, with key witnesses such as Michael Bowker left missing in action. As he observed, Jim Batten could have been five times worse than portrayed and still not deserved to get shot. As Freida Batten said, nothing Jim did was "killworthy." Colleen, in effect, had imposed the death penalty, a one-woman firing squad operating under rule .410. But for the jury, politically correct victim ideology and battered woman syndrome, though not identified as such in court, played a major role in the decision.

"We were aware that a man's life had been taken and we felt his death should have been investigated," jury foreman Paul Laufman told the *Mountain Democrat*. Friends and relatives of Jim Batten found were also "aware" that a man's life had been taken, and who had done the taking. And as they knew, the jury did not deliberate to rule whether Jim Batten's death "should have been investigated." When someone guns down a man with a shotgun, police do tend to investigate.

"But the net result," Laufman added, "was that we felt there was insufficient proof of intent to commit murder."

Relatives and friends of Jim Batten might have wondered if Laufman and his fellow jurors had been paying attention. Pointing a loaded shotgun at someone signals intent, and the defendant had done that twice. At close range, she carefully aimed both shotgun blasts to hit vital organs. As forensic pathologist Robert Anthony had testified, both shots were lethal. No impartial observer would consider the two shots an attempt to injure.

Laufman did not suffer from amnesia and some 30 years later told CBS news he remembered the case very vividly. Asked if Colleen Batten seemed like a killer, he said, "No, she didn't to most of us. She seemed very engaging with people." When the jurors returned from lunch, he said, "she was standing at the door smiling at us as we came in and it looked cordial."

The jury had not convened to assess whether Colleen Batten looked cordial but whether she committed murder.

"We had some misgivings," Laufman said. "Our only option was first degree or free, acquittal."

As it happens, the court's minute order for February 6 clearly states that the jury found the defendant not guilty of both first-degree murder and second-degree murder. But as reporters asked, were they setting free a killer?

"Well, of course you have to think about that," Laufman said. "But on balance you have to say are we sending an innocent party to jail and premeditation simply was not proved."

Friends and relatives of Jim Batten had grounds for objection. As judges explain to juries, premeditation does not have to be lengthy and can happen quickly. Second-degree murder, as it happens, does not require premeditation. So the jury, as the foreman explained, believed her story that she acted in self-defense. They had seen her weep on the stand, and if her courtroom performance was an act, Laufman said, "It was a very good act."

In reality, that was matter of opinion. For some observers the defendant's testimony was like something from a bodice ripper, full of trap doors and escape hatches, but the jury bought it. In their view, Colleen Ann Batten was a martyr and victim, not a murderer. She made no post-verdict statement to the press but David Weiner was jubilant. He had essentially won the case in jury selection.

"I think it was fair," the attorney said. "During this case I have come to know this lady very well, and she's one fine person." On last day of closing arguments, he said, "I saw her smile" for first time since the killing occurred. "I think good things are in her future now. It was pretty tough for her and the children" with the circumstances "put on a table on Main Street, but it might prove to be the best therapy for them." So they had all been victims.

Since the case ended in acquittal, that meant no victim impact statements from Jim Batten's loved ones. Freida Batten had some things she wanted to say. Jim's niece Diane Barrett believed from the start that he had been murdered. Terry Stone and his siblings also missed their day in court.

Meanwhile, down on Main Street, bars like the Liar's Bench were buzzing over the case. More than a few in Placerville, including those who had known Jim Batten, thought the jury got it wrong, and regarded Dr. Tresser's theory as a brand of psychogenic mendacity. It did not emerge how much the defense had paid Dr. Tresser, or whether he took part in the victory celebrations, but as Weiner told reporters in 2003, it was money well spent.

"Because she had no recollection, the prosecution could not even cross-examine her on what her thoughts were, or what she did, and so forth, so they had a real problem establishing a mental state of mind, which is malice aforethought." After testimony that she suffered from amnesia, Weiner said, "the prosecution was pretty much left without the ability to prove anything more than manslaughter." And Judge Fogerty had disallowed the introduction of a manslaughter charge.

David Weiner won the victory for his client, and that gave his career a boost. Around Placerville, as a friend of Jim Batten put it, the word was, "if you kill somebody, get Weiner." And the attorney's prediction of good things in Colleen's future turned out to be right.

She inherited all Jim Batten's property and took over his surveying business, mapping out a neighborhood of a dozen homes off Pleasant Valley Road near Diamond Springs. She also performed legal work for David Weiner in his Cameron Park office.

In her mid-40s in 1986, Colleen was still trim and attractive, but suitors did not exactly come running, candy and flowers in hand. For some eligible men, the murder trial functioned as a background check, but in due time another man would find his way into Colleen's life.

"He had heart trouble and died."

In 1940, Adolf Hitler's National Socialist forces, then allied with Josef Stalin's USSR, controlled most of Europe but the United States had yet to become involved in the conflict. That same year, the Assistant Fire Chief in Oakland, California, was Thomas Harris. On February 3, 1940, his wife Bernice gave birth to a son, Robert Edward Harris, baptized on March 24 at St. Mary's church. Robert attended Catholic schools from grades 6 to 12 and excelled in religion classes, earning an award at graduation. He was also active in sports and Boy Scouts and all through high school worked a part-time job six days a week.

This schedule left little time for dating, though by one account, at age 15 while on vacation in northern California's Humboldt County, he met Colleen Yates. Back in Oakland, as the story goes, they hooked up and went to a movie. Nothing came of it, and Bob, a top-tier student, moved on to UC Berkeley, the most prized campus in the University of California system, where he majored in civil engineering. The rigorous course schedule and part-time work left little time for social life and dating. In Oakland, Bob met Karen Aylward and they married in 1962, the same year Colleen married Larry Dodge.

Bob and Karen Harris lived in Elgin, Illinois, until 1967, when Bob began working for the U.S. Forest Service. That job took him to Placerville, Redding, San Diego, Grass Valley, and Davis, all in California. It was the ideal state and a dream career for the backpacker, fisherman, and conservationist.

Karen bore three children, Andy, Pamela, and Scott, all high achievers. Scott earned a PhD in sociology from the University of Oregon and wound up teaching at Saint Louis University. Andy is an attorney in Grass Valley, and Pam, a criminal justice major at Chapman University, became a detective with the Los Angeles Police Department. As the children were growing up, Bob and Karen were growing apart. They separated in 1987, when living in Davis and Bob commuting to Pleasanton. After nearly 25 years of marriage, the couple finally divorced in 1988. Bob remained an ambitious man.

The Berkeley grad pushed himself to earn a master's degree in public administration from the University of Southern California. He duly became the administrator of the Lake Tahoe Basin Management Unit, one of the most coveted positions in the U.S. Forest Service. In that role Bob Harris was instrumental in restoring the Pope House, Valhalla and Camp Richardson, and helped with the Tahoe Rim Trail. Bob Harris was a major player in the installation of the Taylor Creek Stream Profile Chamber, with a walkway giving visitors a view of salmon in the creek. In his time with the Forest Service, Bob Harris also headed multidisciplinary teams of recreation planners, landscape architects, hydrologists, and even archeologists. He became a leader with federal, state and county agencies and worked with "externals" including the Job Corps, state fire personnel, honor inmates, and the Civilian Conservation Corps. He also had dealings with Native American groups, the US Navy, and even the offices of the President and the Vice President.

According to Don Lane of the Forest Service, "Bob was known for his love for Lake Tahoe and for his passion to bring consensus to the agencies managing the Tahoe Basin."

It was all part of a job he loved, in a place he loved, but not the limit of his activities. Bob Harris loved baseball and twice served as an umpire for the Little League World Series. In California he umpired little league, high school, and college baseball. At all levels, he proved popular with his colleagues.

At a doubleheader in Auburn, rookie umpire Randy Parker recalled having "two very bad games" with "many rookie mistakes." Parker had yelled "strike!" before the batter hit the ball for a double. On another pitch he raised his right hand to signal a strike but yelled "ball." And on the bases, by his own count, he blew at least five calls, and Parker was certain that the more experienced Bob Harris was going to rake him over the coals. After the game Parker rushed to the parking lot for a quick escape but Harris caught up with him just as he was getting in the car, reminding the rookie that they were supposed to conduct a post-game critique.

As Parker braced himself for the worst, Bob Harris said "Randy, what do you think *I* could do to improve?"

Parker was dumfounded and drove home, "like I had just finished umpiring the seventh game of the World Series and I had not missed a single pitch!" Parker was so impressed with Harris' humility that he wrote up the story for *Referee Magazine*.

Though divorced from Karen, Bob Harris remained a major force in the lives of his children and grandchildren. He played golf with son Andy and grandson Gabe. He played baseball with Pam's children Cole, Quinn and Danica, who knew him as Grandpa Big Bear. When granddaughter Karly pitched softball for her college team in Los Angeles, Bob would show up to watch her.

Around 1985 Bob acquired a cabin in Lake Tahoe. He would go skiing with Pam and her husband Phil, and on visits to their home in South Pasadena he built a playhouse in the back yard, a project he also pulled off for Andy and Scott. He was adept at fixing things and found time to restore a vintage MG and an Austin Healey Sprite. He liked to watch football on television but remained a bigger fan of his children, who never hesitated to seek him out for advice. As the children knew him, he was a man who found the good in people, with respect for the elderly, and generous with all.

In the late 1980s Bob Harris' work sometimes took him to the El Dorado County offices in Placerville. On one of these trips, in January of 1988, he encountered Colleen Batten, whom he had known as a teenager in Oakland. Now in their forties, the two began to see each other socially and during one dinner, Bob's mother Bernice asked Colleen what happened to her second husband.

"He had heart trouble and died," Colleen said. Bernice, a woman of some experience, found that account just a bit too brief. So Bernice and Bob's sister Nancy Glaiberman paid a visit to the El Dorado County Library and reviewed the *Mountain Democrat* accounts of the 1986 murder trial such as the "Colleen Batten – Murderess or Martyr?" story from January 31, 1986. "Although she is accused of shooting her husband in the chest with a shotgun," it read, "then ejecting the fired shell, loading another shotgun shell into the chamber and shooting him a second time through the heart, Colleen Batten sat calmly through the first four days of her trial."

So Colleen's first husband Jim Batten had not simply developed heart trouble and died. Bob Harris did not tell Pam, Scott and Andy about the shotgun death of Jim Batten, but Bernice duly broke the news to Andy, the eldest. When Andy approached his father, Bob explained that Colleen had experienced a hard life. The shooting was "unfortunate," he explained, but Bob told his son he loved Colleen and wanted to provide for her. Beyond that, he didn't care to discuss the matter.

On September 2, 1990, Bob Harris married Colleen. She reportedly tapped her closest friend to cater the event, cooking lasagna, Colleen's favorite food, and baking two wedding cakes. And Colleen Ann Harris would become something of an item in the community. She served on the Ambassadors Council of the El Dorado County Chamber of Commerce, and appeared at ribbon-cutting ceremonies, such as the opening of the Missouri Flat Road overpass, in dresses of 1860s vintage she had made herself. One diaphanous lavender outfit boasted a thick flowered waistband, complimented with a flowery hat, cocked to one side and with earrings to match. Similarly attired, she became a candidate in the El Dorado Rose competition, a unique pageant "for mature women." She was a member of the Shakespeare Club and a cribbage player of some note. As David Weiner predicted in 1986, good things were ahead for her.

After their 1990 marriage, the couple lived in Folsom, down the hill from Placerville and home to the famous prison, along with high-tech companies such as Intel.

Colleen's father Irish Yates died in 2003 and the couple moved into the 3248 Wilderness Way residence, with its ample rear deck and sprawling, neatly landscaped back yard, with a shed and gazebo. It was a good fit for his job in Lake Tahoe, where he still owned a cabin.

In 1997, after 30 years with the U.S. Forest Service, Bob Harris duly retired, as his peers marked the departure with a ceremony. But the UC Berkley grad with the masters from USC did not become inactive.

He hooked up with El Dorado County's STAR program, the Sheriff's Team of Active Retirees. As the County explains it, the trained volunteers "enhance vital crime prevention services and community awareness" and "function as eyes and ears of the department and any suspicious activity is immediately reported to the Sheriff's Office." Colleen, clad in a neat blue suit, posed with Sheriff Jeff Neves and Bob at his STAR graduation in September of 2007. Bob was also a member of the nonprofit Sons in Retirement (SIR) and active with the local church and Knights of Columbus. Bob continued to umpire baseball and when not so occupied, worked around the property and kept his vintage cars in good running condition. And he did not let his conservation work slide.

Bob Harris worked with TBI, the Tahoe Baikal Institute, where his Lake Tahoe experience served him well with devotees of Lake Baikal, the deepest lake in the world. Bob also became active with MEC, the Mongol Ecology Center, and traveled to that region. But Grandpa Big Bear reserved plenty of time for visits to his children and grandchildren. Colleen's children were a different story.

Tawnie married Alan Burton in November of 1981 and they divorced in 1984. Other marriages followed, including one to Brian Black that produced two children. Colleen's son Wesley, still using the Batten surname, avoided family events, so Bob did not see much of him. Debbie lived close by and in 2010, her first husband Jon "Chris" Schenberger was arrested and charged with 109 counts of lewd and lascivious acts with a child under 14 years old. In September, 2011, Schenberger became inmate A16935 at Salinas Valley Prison in Soledad, California. Bob Harris found this kind of drama unsettling. He also discovered that Colleen's falsehoods and embellishments were a standing joke with family and friends.

Bob Harris noted that Colleen's relationship with her father was rather strained. Irish Yates did not appear to like her much, perhaps because of what he knew about the killing of Jim Batten. When Irish passed away in 2003, Colleen charged that his wife Helen, who was not Colleen's mother, had poisoned him and forced her to leave the house on Wilderness Way.

That year Tawnie, then married to Brian Black, sought a restraining order against her own mother. In a sworn statement, Tawnie said that her mother had pulled guns on people and bragged that she could fool any counselor. In the matter of Tawnie and Jim Batten, Colleen had said

"If you weren't such a slut it never would have happened." A judge did not grant the restraining order, but Tawnie remained estranged from her mother. The antics of Colleen's children, meanwhile, were not the only trouble spot for Bob Harris.

Colleen was "not a greedy person," David Weiner told the jury in 1986, but Bob Harris had reason to be skeptical. His wife duly inherited Jim Batten's property but learned she was eligible for more, courtesy of the man she had killed in 1985. In 2004, nearly 20 years later, Colleen turned 62 and became eligible for Social Security. She was eligible for Jim Batten's benefits but to receive the money, the rules stipulated, she could not be married. So Colleen proposed that she and Bob divorce then remarry. Bob objected that this was a scam but eventually went along with her plan to get survivor benefits courtesy of Jim Batten. He and Colleen divorced and Colleen duly began receiving monthly benefits of some $1,100. Then Bob and Colleen remarried but for Bob the episode revealed the dark side of his reality. He was married to a woman whose own children called her a fabricator, and worse. He was married to a woman who had killed her second husband. And that husband had not, as Colleen had told Bob's mother Bernice, simply developed heart trouble and died.

Tawnie remained at odds with her mother for some ten years but on New Year's Day, 2012, she duly appeared asking for forgiveness. Bob Harris was not pleased with this development. Colleen had let slip that Tawnie had in fact been in love with Jim Batten, and had been devastated when Jim and Colleen separated. That was a different version of events than what had emerged in the 1986 trial.

In July of 2012, Colleen's first husband Larry Dodge passed away at the age of 69 in Dallas, Texas. As the *Dallas Morning News* put it, "he was a brilliant, kind, generous, and caring man who touched many lives with his knowledge, his friendship, and his love of life, freedom, and people." Obituaries mentioned Dodge's daughters Deborah and Tawnie, but nothing about a son named Wesley. So his father's true identity remained a matter of some mystery.

In addition to professorships in New York and Montana, Dr. Lawrence Burnham Dodge had enjoyed success as a professional photographer and songwriter. An activist with the Libertarian Party, he co-founded the Fully Informed Jury Association. Dodge was a sociologist, not a lawyer, and how he developed interests in that area is uncertain. It is not beyond a reasonable doubt that the Batten case was a factor. That case was also wearing on Colleen's current husband, Bob Harris.

From June to September of 2012 he had been in Mongolia, where he struck up a relationship with a Mongolian graduate student. That enraged Colleen, who texted his daughter Pamela about it incessantly. Emotionally she was all over the map, with sadness giving way to anger. She would say that Bob has a year to decide what he wants to do. But she would also say, "I'm not going to let a younger lady steal my husband from me."

That same month, Pam Stirling flew up at Bob's request to move his belongings out of the Wilderness Court house and up to the Lake Tahoe cabin. Bob explained he was going to be moving away from Colleen and into his Lake Tahoe residence. The father and his daughter, with whom he was very close, were concerned what Colleen might do.

"Are you sure that she doesn't have any guns?" Pam asked.

Her father said that, as far as he knew, there were no guns at the house. Even so, Bob took the precaution of putting extra locks on the doors of his Tahoe cabin. But when Colleen was recovering from hip surgery, Bob came back down the hill to give her a hand. At Thanksgiving, 2012, family from both sides showed up, including Pam, her husband Phil. Bob Harris duly introduced Wesley to Ono Batkhuu, founder of the Mongol Ecology Center, and Wesley began to share Bob's environmental concerns for Lake Baikal, Lake Hovsgol, and Mongolia in general. This new enthusiasm recalled Wesley's wilderness outings with his first stepfather Jim Batten.

For her part, Colleen was on the mend and by Christmas again able to walk in high heels. During the holiday season she visited Andy's family in Grass Valley and Pam's residence in South Pasadena. To Bob's grandchildren, Colleen had become known as "Grandma Cokey."

On January 1, 2013, Bob's family and friends sent their wishes for a happy new year, but it didn't turn out that way.

"A fatal gunshot wound."

On the first weekend of the year, Sunday, January 6, at approximately 6 p.m., the Eldorado County Sheriff received a 911 call from David Weiner, Colleen's attorney in the 1986 murder trial. Weiner reported a homicide at a home in the 3200 block of Wilderness Court. According to a Sheriff's department press release, "Upon their arrival, deputies met with Colleen Harris, and shortly thereafter, entered the home and located a deceased male. The male victim appeared to have sustained a fatal gunshot wound." The male victim was Robert E. Harris, 72, and police arrested his wife Colleen. She went through a medical checkup at Marshall Hospital, followed by an interview with detectives, in which she appeared confused. In her account, her husband had a "bloody nose" and she had put a heavy blanket over him so he would not get cold. Detectives explained that her husband was in fact dead.

"Oh, my God," she told them. "You're joking, right?"

The detectives weren't joking. Bob Harris was dead.

"On or about the 6th day of January, 2013," the January 9 El Dorado County criminal complaint alleged, "the crime of MURDER, in violation of Penal Code Section 187 (a) was committed by COLLEEN ANN HARRIS, who did unlawfully, and with malice aforethought murder Robert Harris, a human being." The complaint further alleged "that in the commission of the foregoing offense, the defendant COLLEEN HARRIS, personally used a firearm, to wit: a 12-gauge shotgun, within the meaning of Section 122022.53(b) of the Penal Code."

The language was practically identical to the 1985 case charging the murder of Jim Batten. This time the court was more specific with the shotgun, "a 12-gauge." And the victim carried a higher profile. On January 15, 2013, the Eldorado County Supervisors adjourned their meeting in honor of Robert Harris. The Amador-El Dorado Forest Forum and TBI also honored him after his death.

As the criminal complaint said, the murder victim had been Robert Harris, "a human being." At the funeral on January 18, fellow umpire Randy Parker sought to illuminate just what kind of human being Bob Harris had been.

"My name is Randy Parker, and Bob Harris was my friend," he said.

On Sunday, January 6, Parker had been sitting in church listening to a message about encouragement. "Little did I know," Parker said, "that my friend, one of the *best* I've known at encouraging me, Bob Harris, was meeting God, face-to-face, for the very first time." And this would bring on "one of the loudest and longest standing ovations in the history of heaven." That was deserved because "Bob's ability to keep those around him *encouraged* was one of his greatest gifts."

Then Parker told the story about how, after his bad performance at the Auburn doubleheader, his friend Bob Harris had asked him, "Randy, what do you think *I* could do to improve?" That was what kind of human being he was.

In the guest book, Al Todd of Annapolis Maryland wrote that his Forest Service boss Bob Harris "treated others with honesty, respect, kindness, and a good sense of humor." He was "a truly wonderful person who will be sorely missed."

Dick Silberberger of Claremont, California had worked with Bob in the Shasta Trinity National Forest and known him as a friend for 44 years. "When you first met Bob," Silberberger wrote, "he immediately made you feel that he would be a friend for life, which in my case certainly turned out to be true."

Bruce Mangan of Paradise, California, wrote that Bob was always friendly and "willing to help you or guide you through troubled times." Lorraine Gerchas, who had known Bob in the Forest Service, wrote, "our family is heartbroken to have lost this very special person in our lives."

Lisa O'Daly of South Lake Tahoe recalled a man "very kind and smart," and one who had touched many lives.

As friends paid tribute, the hills around Placerville were alive with stories about Bob's wife.

"Woman charged with murder in 3rd husband's death," headlined a story from Sacramento's KXTV News 10. "It's a déjà vu murder case in El Dorado County court," the article said. "A Placerville woman acquitted almost 30 years ago for killing her second husband is now charged with killing her third husband."

El Dorado County sheriff deputies arrested Colleen Harris on Sunday, January 6 "after her husband Robert Harris, 72, was found dead inside her Wilderness Court home." The KXTV article also noted that Harris was previously charged with murder and for her second husband's shooting death in 1985, when "Sheriff deputies found the body of James Roger Batten beaten and shot in their home."

"This is Harris' second time as a defendant in a murder case," the *El Dorado Hills Telegraph* reported. "In the previous incident, Harris reportedly called law enforcement to inform them that her then-husband, James Batten, was dead. During that trial she claimed she had amnesia and didn't recall what had happened. Harris was acquitted of the killing."

In her booking photo, her pale, lined face contrasted the dark dyed hair and the bright orange jail garb. To those of a certain age, she could have appeared a morose and slightly malevolent Ma Kettle, or perhaps Granny in "The Beverly Hillbillies." Her rather blank expression betrayed no sense of surprise, perhaps because she had been jailed and charged with murder before.

"The prior incident has ZERO relevance to the current action," her attorney said in papers filed with the court, "especially in light of the fact that Mrs. Harris was ACQUITTED of the charge."

As it happened, the "prior incident" would have a great deal of relevance, but it also presented issues of access. According to California law, in cases of acquittal, the transcript of the trial may be tossed after ten years. That was indeed the fate of the 1986 Batten transcript, reporters were told. El Dorado County prosecutors even tracked down the court reporter of the time, only to find she no longer possessed the transcript. On the other hand, the current case suffered no shortage of physical evidence.

"She killed her prior husband with a shotgun."

The District Attorney can make the call to hold a preliminary hearing or bring the case before a grand jury. A preliminary hearing allows cross-examination and prosecutors can gain a sense of the defense's strategy. They knew Colleen Harris had been tried in 1986 for killing her husband Jim Batten with a shotgun. She was retaining the same attorney, David Weiner, whom the DA's office knew well. That gave prosecutors advance warning of the defense strategy, so they opted for the grand jury.

Deputy District Attorney Joe Alexander handled the proceedings on Monday, June 24, 2013. His first witness was LAPD detective Pamela Stirling, who had met him on January 8 when he walked her through the crime scene on Wilderness Court where her father had been killed.

"Ms. Stirling, to begin with, can you tell me your relationship to a person named Robert or Bob Harris?"

"I'm his daughter."

"Okay. And are you familiar with a person named Colleen Ann Harris?"

"Yes."

"And who is she?"

"That was my dad's wife."

"Is she your mother?"

"No."

"Stepmother?"

"Correct."

"How long was she married to your father?"

58

"23 years."

Stirling said her father and Colleen had met in 1987, married in 1990, and the witness charted their various residences, most recently at 3248 Wilderness Court.

"Were you aware of or did anyone ever report to you that there was any sort of domestic violence between your father and your stepmother?"

"No."

"And do you recall was there ever any reports or anyone ever tell you there was violence between your father and mother during the time they were married?"

"No."

"And what was your father's nature like? Was he a temperamental man, a violent man or was he calm?"

"Very gentle soul, good, loving Catholic, nice, sweet man."

"What about weapons, did you ever know him to own or possess weapons, particularly firearms?"

"I didn't know him to have one. However, he told me that he had a small .22, I believe it was, that he had in Tahoe but it had gone missing about seven, eight years ago. And he had no idea how it went missing."

"Do you remember that .22 he described to you, did he describe it as a revolver or handgun or rifle?"

"A small gun, a small handgun. I don't know."

"And why was it – you said that he, your father, told you that the gun went missing seven or so years ago, seven or eight years ago. When is it that you had that conversation with him about the location of that firearm?"

"I was going with him to move stuff out of the house from Wilderness," Stirling said. "He wanted to move out of the house into the Tahoe house. He owned a house in Tahoe. And I was driving with him to the Wilderness house and I asked him if there were any guns in the house."

Bob Harris wanted to move into his Tahoe house, Stirling told the grand jury, because he wanted to leave Colleen. He was "real tired of dealing with all the drama" in Colleen's family which "just had one problem after the other. And it just started to really wear on him and caused a lot of turmoil in his life that was unnecessary. And then his feelings for Colleen were not the same."

Stirling also explained that her father had established a relationship with a woman in Mongolia, and how that provoked Colleen.

"It was all she talked about," Stirling testified. "She was all over the map. She was sad, she cried and she was sad. And then she would get angry. And then she would say he has a year to decide what he wants to do and then I'm leaving him. Then she would go to 'I'm not going to let a younger lady steal my husband from me.'" Her emotions, Stirling said, were "all over the map."

"Did you ever know Colleen to have a shotgun?" Alexander asked.

"No."

"Did she ever talk to you about her ability to shoot guns or familiarity with guns?"

"Yes. She used to live in the woods in, I don't remember, Montana or something. She lived in the woods and she would shoot animals for her food."

"In fairness, you have no idea whether she was telling a story?"

"I have no idea."

"Okay," Alexander said. "But she did tell you that, and from that you inferred she had some familiarity or comfort with firearms?"

"Yes."

Alexander probed the issue further.

"Why were you and your father feeling afraid that it might be dangerous to go to the Wilderness Court house in September 2012, when you were going up to collect some of your father's belongings?"

"Because she killed her prior husband with a shotgun," Stirling said.

"And you're aware she was acquitted of that?"

"I am."

The members of the grand jury were now aware as well.

Stirling stepped down and Alexander called El Dorado County sheriff's deputy Michael Roberts. On January 6 he had been dispatched to investigate a homicide. Roberts had been one of the last officers to arrive and it was "pitch black." The house is "out in the woods," he said, and sits on a hill. Police set up a staging area at the foot of the driveway.

"Several of us in two patrol cars responded to the front of the house, illuminated the front with spotlights," Roberts said. "We advised our dispatch to make a phone call into the residence and ask that anybody inside come outside with nothing in their hands."

"Okay," said Alexander. "And did someone come out of that house?"

"Yes."

"Can you describe that person?"

"Yes. She was identified as Colleen Harris. She was an elderly female, approximately 70 years old, long, straight hair."

Alexander asked Roberts how he had proceeded.

"I asked her what had happened," he said. "At which point she stated something along the lines she couldn't talk about it. I then let her know that it was indicated to us that somebody may be inside the house either injured or deceased. She confirmed there was. I asked who was inside the house. She said her husband. I asked if anybody else had access to the residence or anybody else lived there, at which point she said no, it was just her and her husband. And then I began to ask her – you know, it appeared to me she knew more than what she was saying, so I said, look, I have to go inside the house. I want to make sure it's safe for me and my partners to go in. You've got to give me something to work with."

"What happened?"

"She again stated she couldn't talk about it. And I said, well, at least tell me how he died or I'm sorry, she did confirm that her husband was deceased. I asked how he died. I said was he shot, was he stabbed, did he fall down, what? And then she responded by saying he's been shot."

"Did she say whether she had done anything to cover him up or anything?"

"Yes, she did. I asked her if she confirmed, how did she confirm he was deceased, whether she checked a pulse or checked for breathing? And she said she covered him up, at which point she said he looked beautiful."

Roberts had yet to see the victim, and after he did, the statement about the victim looking beautiful struck him as "very odd."

Alexander asked Roberts what he saw inside the house.

"We had made our way back to a master bedroom," Roberts said, "which going through the front door was down a hallway at the very end to the right, the bedroom door on the left of the hallway. When I opened up the door, in the middle of the room is a bed. It was obvious to me, I could see that there was more than likely a person lying in bed underneath the covers. My partners branched out to the right and left to ensure no suspects were inside the house, at which point I approached the bed and pulled down the blankets, at which point I saw the victim lying in bed."

"And can you describe what you saw?"

"Yes," Roberts said. "He was missing the majority of his face. There was a shotgun down by his left leg. His head was tilted slightly to the right. There was a large hole behind his ear and I could see inside his skull. It was obvious he was deceased. There was a lot of blood and spatter, I would say, to the victim's right toward the bedroom window."

"When you were talking to Colleen outside the residence," Alexander said, "did she describe to you the weapon that had caused the injuries to her husband?"

"Yes. I asked her what type of weapon it was, she said she didn't know. I asked if it was a rifle type or a long rifle or shotgun or a handgun, she said she didn't know. So then I asked her to show me how long it was, at which point, using her hands, this isn't going to be on the audio or anything, but using her hands she said about this big" he said, demonstrating with his hands, "which I estimated about three feet in length."

"Is that consistent with the shotgun you found there?"

"Yes."

Roberts stepped down and Alexander called Cameron Jones, an El Dorado County sheriff's deputy and the lead CSI investigator in the case. Alexander showed Jones some crime scene photos, including the victim in bed and a close-up of the gunshot wound to his head.

"Based on your training and experience," Alexander said, "did that appear to be a shotgun wound to you?"

"Yes," Jones said, and noted that the victim's right arm was tucked under the pillow. He also identified photos of the victims left side, and of the shotgun that was at the lower right-hand edge of the bed.

"Is that the position it was in when you arrived at the scene?"

"Yes," Jones said. "The shotgun was not moved. There was a gray sheet or something partially covering that that was moved so that we could take a better picture of the gun."

"When you first arrived, the body was still covered by bedding, blankets and sheets?"

"Yes."

Several deputies were with him when they started removing those items so they could see the body, and detective Mike Lensing was also in the room.

"While you were removing blankets and the bedding from the bed to get down to the victim as he laid in place, did you note anything unusual about the blood or bodily material that was on the bed?"

"It appeared that there was some apparent blood material on the sheets underneath the gray sheet or the gray blanket that was there."

"What did you conclude from that?"

"That the gray blanket had been placed there after the gunshot wound had occurred."

Jones told the jurors he found no evidence that the body had been moved, no evidence of a struggle, and no evidence of a forced entry. The victim's wallet, credit card, check books and other items of value were still in place and "nothing had appeared to have been touched."

Alexander asked Jones to describe damage from the shotgun blast.

"Over on the floor to the right side of the bed there were several piece of material blown on top of the fan blade. There was what looked like pieces of flesh and hair all over the ceiling. And this is everything on the right side of the bedroom where, from the investigation, it looked like the gunshot originated from."

"So this would be an area where the gun was located when the trigger was pulled?"

"Yes."

But Jones saw nothing on the left hand or arm, and said this was consistent with the idea that the victim's left side was covered with a sheet or blanket at the time of the shot. And Jones saw nothing to indicate that the right arm was in any other position at the time the shot was inflicted.

"If his arm moved," Alexander said, "you would expect to see blood smear or seepage or something like that?"

"Yes."

"You didn't see anything like that?"

"No."

Jones concluded that the entrance wound was "in proximity to the rear of the left ear."

"And the exit wound, is all that damage we see to his right side, so the right side of his face, from his perspective?"

"Yes."

"Did you note anything else about the blood spatter as you continued examining this scene?"

Jones said that on the ceiling "it looked like some of the blood had been disturbed and almost like someone had started to wipe then stopped." The smear marks were directly over the bed, Jones said, and "it looked like someone had taken some sort of cloth or paper towel or something and begun to wipe and then stopped."

"Is that consistent with the idea that after this gunshot was inflicted, there was some attempt to clean up the scene?"

"Very brief, yes," Jones said. "Very brief attempt."

"And based on your observations at the scene and the amount of blood and tissue that was spattered about the room, and in particular on the bedding and the pillow where the decedent was laying, would it have been very difficult to actually clean up this scene?"

"I would say it would have been almost impossible."

Alexander wanted to know if the attempt to clean up the scene had been limited to the area on the ceiling. Jones said it was, and found no other evidence of attempts to clean up the scene. The victim, he said, had not been dead when he was shot, and Jones saw nothing to indicate the body had been moved.

"Based on your observations," Alexander said, "did you form an opinion as to whether or not this was a homicide or suicide?"

"Based on my training and experience, I would conclude this was a homicide."

"What do you base that on?"

"I've been to numerous suicides and I've been to several other instances where there's been an accidental discharge of a firearm, and this is nothing like any of those."

If the decedent had been the one who pulled the trigger, Jones said, there would have been obvious marks on his hand, and Jones found none. The way the blood had congealed around him, and the lividity, the blood settling at the bottom of the body, all showed that the victim remained in place after he had been shot.

Deputy Anthony Prencipe identified a photo of the shotgun and gave its serial number, 80-51817A. He did not check whether it was a registered weapon. Detective Natashia Gallagher, who took photographs of Colleen Harris, testified that she had complained of chest pains and had "a dark spot between her breasts." Gallagher had been trained with 12-gauge shotguns and testified that they pack a powerful recoil. The bruising she saw on Colleen Harris, she testified, was consistent with a shotgun kicking back and striking her in the chest.

Alexander called Mike Lensing, a detective of ten years experience who had been on the scene at Wilderness Court. He told the grand jury of his training in crime scene investigation and recognition as a expert in blood spatter.

Alexander asked Lensing what he observed as the sheets were being removed from the victim.

"The bedding consisted of a dark-colored blanket that was located over the top of the victim. And I noticed that the dark-colored blanket did not have any blood spatter on the outside of the blanket. That blanket was placed in that location after the fatal incident occurred. Upon removing that blanket, I could see the blanket below, which was the comforter to the bed, had an even spread of blood spatter, little bit of brain matter and some tissue on top of the blanket. So that indicates that that comforter was what was exposed at the time the fatal incident occurred. At that time I noticed the sheets were up to the top of the bed and there was even spatter all the way across. The decedent's hands or left hand was underneath this blanket, therefore, not exposed. The decedent's right hand was under the pillow also not exposed. Once the sheets or the upper blanket was pulled back, there was no blood spatter or blood deposited underneath the sheet. Again proof that the sheet with the blood spatter on it was on and up to the decedent's upper chest portion at the time of the fatal incident."

Lensing found no spatter on the left arm and only a bit on the right arm, at the elbow. Based on his observations, "the decedent did not shoot himself" and a blanket had been placed over the victim "a significant amount of time later" because "there was no blood spatter transfer."

Alexander wanted to know what led Lensing to believe that it was not a self-inflicted gunshot wound. "With a suicide you're going to have a contact wound," he said, and the wound and power marks did not square with that. "With a shotgun that is longer, it is very difficult to hold it away from your face to be able to have that occur."

Lensing found that the shotgun was out of the decedent's reach, and placed on some blood spatter that had already dried. Lensing also found that "in the middle of the pattern of blood spatter were smear marks you could see as if somebody had wiped or tried to wipe some of the blood spatter away."

Lensing found no evidence of forced entry and no sign of struggle in the house.

The decedent looked to be in a position of rest and "It just looked as if this incident of violence occurred without him even knowing."

Lensing and his partner Paul Hadjes had interviewed Colleen Harris.

"And did Ms. Harris appear to be sober while you were talking to her?"

"Yes."

"Did she appear to have any mental health issues or problems communicating with you?"

"No problems communicating with me. I don't know what her mental health status was at the time. She appeared to be normal."

"Essentially did she answer your questions? Was she on topic when you asked a question? Did she give you an answer appropriate for the question you asked?"

"Yes."

"Didn't appear confused or dazed or anything of that nature?"

"No."

"Did you ask her what had happened that day?"

"Yes."

"What did she say?"

"She stated that she didn't know. Her last memory was on January fifth in the evening, her and her husband had a very nice evening. She thought that they may have had dinner. They sat down and watched television. Her next memory was – she didn't know exactly when this memory occurred – but her next memory was her standing at the bedside of her husband, noticed that he was bleeding, noticed that there was a shotgun on the bed, and didn't think anything of the blood because she said her husband normally had nose bleeds. Then she placed the blanket over the top of him. She then loses memory after that. And her next memory is when our deputy contacted her at her house."

"Did you ask her whether she had killed her husband?"

"Yes."

"What did she say?"

"She stated that she loved him and would never do that."

"Did she say whether or not anyone else was at the house in the last 24 to 48 hours that could have done this?"

"She stated there was nobody there besides herself during this entire time."

"Did she have any explanation for what had happened to her husband?"

"None at all."

"Did you ask her about where that shotgun came from?"

"Yes."

"What did she say?"

"She stated it was a gift from her husband, from the decedent because she had been raped in her home several times. And he had gotten that so she could protect herself when he was away."

"Were you able to find any evidence to corroborate that version of events?"

"The version of events of her being raped?" said Lensing, who also worked as a sexual assault detective. "No, there were no cases."

That is, he clarified, she had not reported any rapes or sexual assault.

"Was she able to provide you with any accounting of what she had done or had been doing during the time frame that her husband was killed?"

"None. She had stated that she never left the house. Nobody came to her house. She never made a phone call and nobody ever called her."

"And did she have any explanation for her inability to remember a large chunk of time during which her husband was killed?"

"No," the detective said. "I had asked her if her loss of memory is something that normally happened or ever happened before. And she says, no, normally I'm of my right mind and never lost my memory."

"Did she have any injuries that you would associate with being knocked unconscious or having a head injury or anything of that nature?"

"None. She seemed to be focused. She was unemotional but she seemed to be focused."

"What do you mean she was unemotional?"

"During the interview we told her – she claimed to not know her husband was dead. We told her that her husband was dead. She knew from the line of questioning that we were looking at her as a suspect in this case. And she never asked why she was there. She never asked any questions. She was just happy, matter of fact she was joking around at times."

"Okay," Alexander said. "Did you ask her whether there was any domestic violence between herself and her husband, Robert Harris?"

"She stated no, there was no violence, and he was a very loving man."

"Did she talk to you at all about her belief that her husband was having an affair with another woman or had a relationship with another woman?"

"No. She did not tell us that. We had found that information out during the interview and we had asked her about that and then she finally said yes, he is having an affair."

"So initially – I want to make sure that we have this correct. Did she initially deny there were any problems in her relationship with her husband Robert Harris?"

"Yes."

"So she denied there were any problems between the two of them?"

"That's correct."

"Did she describe the nature of their relationship?"

"She said it was very loving and they loved each other very much."

During the interview, Lensing had received information about the affair, and asked the suspect about it.

"Her response was yes, he was having an affair. We worked it out. And she is very loving. She understands what had happened. And they are just in the process of working through that and moving on with their relationship."

"And so she believed that there was a reconciliation and they were just going to move on with their relationship as husband and wife?"

"Exactly."

"Did she talk about him moving out or planning to move out?"

"No."

"Did you give her opportunities and ask her more than once about what had happened, did she explain that?"

"Yes," Lensing said. "I gave her numerous chances over the several hours that we interviewed her."

"And she wasn't able to provide any greater detail than what you already told the grand jury about what had happened?"

"No."

"She wasn't able to provide any information about someone else committing this crime?"

"No."

"Did she ever claim or suggest that her husband was unhappy or despondent or killed himself?"

"Never."

"Did she make any claim that he was threatening – if he hadn't committed domestic violence, was he threatening to commit domestic violence on her?"

"No," Lensing said. "They had a pleasant evening, had dinner and were sitting watching TV together."

"And that was the extent of her recollection before it picked up again?"

"Yes."

"And then it picked up again where she is standing at the end of the bed and he's got what she believes to be a bloody nose and the shotgun, and she covers him up and the next recollection is when the sheriff deputies arrive?"

"Yes."

The state had no records of ownership for the shotgun. One chamber was loaded, the other empty. Death had been instantaneous, Lensing said, "because there was no movement of the body once the weapon was discharged. And to reaffirm that, the contents of decedent's skull were evacuated. So there was no brain to allow function of the body afterwards."

No fingerprints had been found on the weapon and firearms expert Mike Franzen found no records that the gun, retailed by Kmart, had been owned or registered to Colleen Harris or Robert Harris.

Franzen testified that such a weapon delivers considerable recoil and could easily kick back and strike a person, causing an injury. Deputy Daryl Miller, who had booked Colleen Harris into the county jail, testified that she identified an injury on the middle finger of her right hand. The injury appeared fresh, but she could not remember how the injury occurred.

Alexander told the grand jury that Mr. Harris had an issue with her husband and that the answers she gave detectives "are inconceivable and inconsistent with the events as we know from the crime scene." There had been attempts to clean up the scene and to delay the reporting of the event.

"The evidence," Alexander said, "particularly the crime scene evidence, seems to lead to the conclusion that he was almost certainly asleep when he was shot. And that he remained in the position he was in from the moment he was shot forward."

Alexander found "no evidence of a struggle. No evidence of a break-in. No evidence of domestic violence. There's no evidence of a self-defense claim. This is the murder of a sleeping person completely unable to defend himself."

Alexander detailed the injuries to the defendant and told the jurors they could consider all the photos.

"And based on the testimony of the witnesses and your own review of the photos," he said, "the cause of death in this particular case is no great mystery. I mean, it's a massive shotgun wound to his head. It's clear that it killed him almost instantaneously."

The evidence pointed to another shotgun wedding. She got herself a shotgun, loaded it up, and killed Bob Harris before he could run. That is, she killed him before he could move out and end their relationship.

The suspect and her attorney would get their chance to clarify matters in the jury trial that lay ahead. The transcript of the 1986 trial was still unavailable, but as it turned out, a dearth of information would not be the only problem.

"Maybe I'll kill him."

Since Colleen Batten's 1986 acquittal, the battered woman defense had colonized the legal system. In 1990, governor Richard Celeste of Ohio granted clemency to 25 women who had murdered their husbands. It was the first such release in U.S. history, hailed by politically correct activists but opposed by prosecutors such as Dennis Watkins who believed it would promote the taking of human life.

"The fact that you're battered does not give you the license to kill," Watkins told reporters. "Now, instead of going to the courts or getting a divorce, these women will think, 'Maybe I'll kill him.'" Some women were indeed battered, Watkins said, but some were making it up.

Brenda Koss of Cleveland shot and killed her husband while he was asleep. In such as case, Ohio prosecutor John Murphy said, battering is not a proper self-defense claim, and "not a proper defense for murder."

In California, governor Pete Wilson granted clemency to Mary Caccavale, who stabbed her spouse to death, and in 1993 reduced the sentence of Brenda Denise Aris, who shot her abusive husband Rick Aris five times while he slept. The Republican governor told reporters, "Although I cannot condone the killing, even of Rick Aris, and the choices made by Ms. Aris on that fatal night, I feel compassion for the woman who is before me today."

That same year, during the Super Bowl, NBC ran an ad claiming that on Super Bowl Sunday violence against women increases 40 percent. In the entire nation, only one reporter, Ken Ringle of the *Washington*

Post, bothered to check the facts. He discovered no evidence that violence against women increases 40 percent on Super Bowl Sunday. The story wasn't true but the activists did not publish a retraction. Instead they attacked Ringle and the politically correct myth lingered on.

In the 1986 trial Colleen Batten had shown no physical signs of abuse and many in the know believed she had made it all up. But Colleen Harris and her attorney David Weiner were not the only ones still around. Peter Hecht of the *Sacramento Bee* tracked down Walter Miller, who prosecuted the case against Colleen Batten.

"I thought she had committed a homicide," Miller said. "I argued sincerely for a conviction for murder." On that point, his memory was clear.

"If you acquit Colleen Batten," Miller told the jury in 1986, "it would be a dire consequence to the system because she murdered Jim Batten." But as Miller told Peter Hecht nearly three decades later, "I can't say I expected her to do it again."

The Harris case drew national and international attention, and Laura Cole of the local CBS station tracked down Paul Laufman, the jury foreman in 1986. Reporters told him that, in similar style, Bob Harris had been gunned down with a shotgun.

"That's gut-wrenching because that person may be alive if we had rendered a different verdict," said Laufman. He explained that the jury had not made a mistake in 1986, but on the other hand, he did have mixed feelings.

"Well, it saddens me, it saddens me, and you think, 'Well, would that person be alive if we had found her guilty?' and the answer is probably yes." Laufman also told Laura Cole, "If 30 years ago that was an act, it was a very good act," and "To me, this is a little too convenient."

Dan McKelvie, a neighbor of Colleen Harris, told Peter Hecht "I'm just blown away by the coincidence," perhaps a strange choice of words, given what had taken place. And McKelvie also recalled the court case about her previous husband. "She was acquitted last time. So I can't say there were two murders." McKelvie knew Colleen as a "very nice person," and as he told the reporter, "It just amazes me what's going on. I feel terrible for her. I don't know what the facts are. I don't want to rush to judgment." Others had already made the call.

Colleen's children showed up at her first court appearance but would not answer questions from reporters. But several people claiming to be Colleen's friends told CBS that she was "physically and emotionally abused by her husband and that she killed him in self-defense." How they knew these realities was not explained, but Colleen's size seemed to work in her favor.

For the CBS reporters, "At 70 years old, it's hard to imagine that a woman so small in stature could be accused of murdering her husband." She had been acquitted before but "now, she awaits trial for the murder of another husband, 72-year-old Robert Harris. And it seems, her new case may have a similar defense." But could another jury reach the same conclusion? CBS posed that question to Jennifer Mouzis, a high-profile local defense attorney and former deputy district attorney for Sacramento County.

"These two separate juries in these two separate cases can absolutely come to the same verdict," Mouzis explained. "If she picked another abusive husband and she felt her life was in danger, she's going to resort to do what she knows how to do, and that is to stop her abuser." According to the attorney, "The chances of anybody getting acquitted on any murder is always very small, but it's also very case specific. So it's going to depend on the facts of this particular case. I've heard she's a very small, slight person. That's going to play a factor in what the jury considers."

So size matters, as the legal expert had it, along with "the facts of this particular case." Those facts, and the earlier case, did not deter Colleen's friends from offering their services as character witnesses in letters to attorney David Weiner.

A Shingle Springs man who had known Colleen for 10 years described her as an "honest, caring and a remarkable person." Colleen "has the compassion and caring many people do not have" and was "someone you looked up to and admired." The friend concluded: "I do believe she needs to be treated with lenience on this obvious injustice done to her." So again, Colleen was the victim.

"I can't imaging what would have driven her to such a drastic situation," wrote a woman who knew Colleen but not Bob. "I just know she is a lovely lady and has so much to offer to the community."

Another woman who knew Colleen for many years, "always found her to be a hardworking, caring, sensitive and intelligent person. She has spent her life giving to others, especially young people." The writer had "no knowledge of this tragic situation," but wrote, "it is my hope that there will be a place in the future for Colleen Harris to utilize her many fine qualities, especially those as a gifted teacher and nurse."

Another woman recalled that Colleen Batten-Harris a fellow El Dorado County Ambassador, had given her a check for $100 when she and her husband were struggling. Colleen "loved her community and was always gentle and kind" and the writer had "never heard her speak a critical or harsh word in all the time I had known her. She was always full of grace, dignity, gentleness and kindness." And the friend wanted to "stand with her" at trial.

The longest character reference came from one of Colleen's oldest friends and her strongest supporter. In her letter to Weiner, she recalled Larry Dodge and Jim Batten, Colleen's first two husbands. In her account, Jim Batten came home after being out all night "held a gun to her head and raped her." Colleen "struggled, got the gun and shot Jim." The friend took her to the court hearings "and she was found NOT GUILTY by a jury and she went on with her life."

Bob Harris "seemed like a nice man but liked to brag about himself and about what he did" even though "Colleen did most of the homework for Bob" when he enrolled in university courses.

"She had three husbands who were all alike," Colleen's friend wrote. "They all had big egos. Colleen worked for them and they took credit. It is my opinion they didn't love her. She was taught by her father to protect herself when threatened. She became the survivor.

"Colleen is a baptized Christian and has read the Bible four times that I know of. She lives by the Golden Rule and obeys all the laws. She has been a worker and caring person her entire life. Unfortunately three husbands have taken advantage of her. All three husbands treated Colleen like a slave."

Colleen's friend concluded, "it is time for Colleen to be a free Woman and live the rest of her life in peace and quiet. She was forced into saving her own life from someone else's WRONG DOINGS."

Out in the community, many noted the similarities between the killings of Jim Batten and Bob Harris, with one key difference. This time the small, slight person accused of murder was not released on bail and would remain in El Dorado County jail as she awaited trial. Before that trial took place, her attorney David Weiner would handle another killing with some eerie similarities.

"Two dead wives."

Todd Winkler, a pharmaceutical company executive and former U.S. Air Force fighter pilot, lived in upscale Cameron Park, a short drive west of Placerville. On the morning of February 27, 2012, Mr. Winkler's neighbor, a lawyer, called the El Dorado County Sheriff's department.

"What's your emergency?" the operator said.

"I'm calling to report a fatality."

"What happened there?"

"My understanding it was a domestic, uh, dispute, fight, confrontation."

At the scene, Mr. Winkler spoke with deputies.

"So where – where is your wife?" an officer said.

"When you enter the house," he said, "you turn to the right, the first bedroom on the right."

"And you're sure she's dead?"

"I'm positive."

"How can you be – how are you sure?"

"No pulse," Mr. Winkler said. "No breathing."

As he told police, he and his wife Rachel were having an argument over custody of the children. He had struck her in anger, and told the officers he was in the process of apologizing when she came at him with a pair of scissors. Police arrested Winkler, who was charged with murder.

The case came to trial in September of 2014 in the courtroom of Superior Court Judge Kenneth Melikian, a Dartmouth College grad who had earned his law degree at the University of Southern

California. Melikian had served as a deputy district attorney in Fresno and San Bernardino Counties, and as Assistant U.S. Attorney for the Eastern District of California. In 2009, California governor Arnold Schwarzenegger appointed Melikian as a judge in El Dorado County. Deputy District Attorney Lisette Suder prosecuted the case and in the early going, with television cameras in the courtroom, Winkler went off on her.

"You do not speak truth. You only want to destroy!" the 47-year-old screamed at Suder, as he attempted to rise from his chair. Bailiff Scott Crawford intervened and cleared the courtroom. When the proceedings resumed, Winkler's attorney David Weiner offered no opening statement, but he had already made his defense clear before the trial. He would argue that Todd Winkler had been treated for "dissociative identity disorder" and had suffered a psychotic episode when he acted in self-defense in the struggle with his wife Rachel.

Several similarities with the 1986 Batten and 2013 Harris cases were evident: The self-defense angle, the claim of psychological disorders, and a lawyer, not the defendant, placing the 911 call. And Judge Melikian allowed the prosecution to take up another familiarity.

Fifteen years earlier, in 1999, Winkler's first wife Catherine Walker died in a car accident in Georgia. As Todd Winkler explained it, she had been rushing him to the hospital after an insect bite when the crash occurred on a remote road. He was ejected from the car and emerged unharmed. Todd Winkler was not charged in the case but recouped an insurance settlement of $1.2 million.

As was his custom, David Weiner put his client on the stand and he testified for more than four hours. Considerable testimony also emerged about him during the four-week trial. Prosecutor Lisette Suder described Winkler as "a mastermind, manipulator and murderer." She showed crime scene photos of Rachel stabbed in the neck, eye, and mouth as she put up her hands to defend herself. She was holding their infant son Alex when Todd returned to finish her off. It was all an act of premeditated murder.

"The defendant has now had two dead wives," Suder told the court. "And in both cases – look at these similarities – he is the only witness." And Rachel's case was not self-defense. "Look at the wounds," Suder told the jury. "That is the evidence, ladies and gentlemen."

For his part, David Weiner was blunt with the jury.

"To find that Todd Winkler killed Catherine Winkler," he said, "you have to rely on wild, blind, idiotic speculation." And in the case of Rachel, Weiner claimed that Todd Winkler's right hand and arm became temporarily paralyzed, as in the case where his client had suffered a nervous breakdown and conversion disorder. Weiner also cited Winkler's amnesia in a shoplifting case when he was in the Air Force.

"This not a murder case, ladies and gentlemen," the attorney said. "This is a self-defense case or – at most – it is a voluntary manslaughter case."

Judge Melikian's option for the jury were first-degree murder, second-degree murder, involuntary manslaughter, and justifiable homicide in self-defense. On October 22, 2014, after deliberating for 22 hours, the jury of seven men and five women found Todd Winkler guilty of first-degree murder.

"I would just say, your honor," Winkler said at the December 8 sentencing. "I feel deep remorse for what's happened, and for Rachel's family, for my family, and especially for my children."

"Mr. Winkler," Judge Melikian said. "You are not the victim in this case. Rachel Winkler is the victim in this case." Then the judge sentenced Todd Winkler to 26 years-to-life for murdering Rachel.

El Dorado County District Attorney Vern Pierson praised Lisette Suder for "bringing this killer to justice." Nothing could bring Rachel back, Pierson said, "But it is my hope that her family, friends and loved ones may find some peace knowing the person responsible for their loss and Rachel's death is being held responsible."

"We knew it was a tough case," Weiner told reporters after the verdict. "We thought those very gruesome things were going to be major, and they were."

As the saying goes around El Dorado County, "if you kill somebody, get Weiner."

Todd Winkler killed somebody. Todd Winkler got Weiner. As of December 17, 2014, Todd Winkler became inmate AV3989 at the California Corrections Center at Susanville.

Meanwhile, in 1985 Colleen Batten had killed someone with a shotgun. She got David Weiner, and David Weiner secured her acquittal.

In 2013 Colleen was arrested for murder, with a shotgun. As in the earlier case, she got Weiner, even before the police knew about the shooting. The veteran attorney, fresh off a defeat, plotted a strategy to get her acquitted a second time.

Airman James Roger Batten, "the best of the Air Force," as a scoutmaster called him, trained downed pilots to survive. (Photo courtesy of Diane Neal-Barrett. Used by permission.)

"He was anchored in this world, and had a great curiosity about its function," says Jim's first wife Freida Batten. (photo by Terry Stone. Used by permission.)

Jim Batten and adopted son Wesley, rafting on the Snake River in Idaho.
(Photo courtesy of Michael Bowker. Used by permission.)

On July 31, 1985, Placerville got the news.
(Lloyd Billingsley photo.)

In old Hangtown, they just didn't know.
(Lloyd Billingsley photo.)

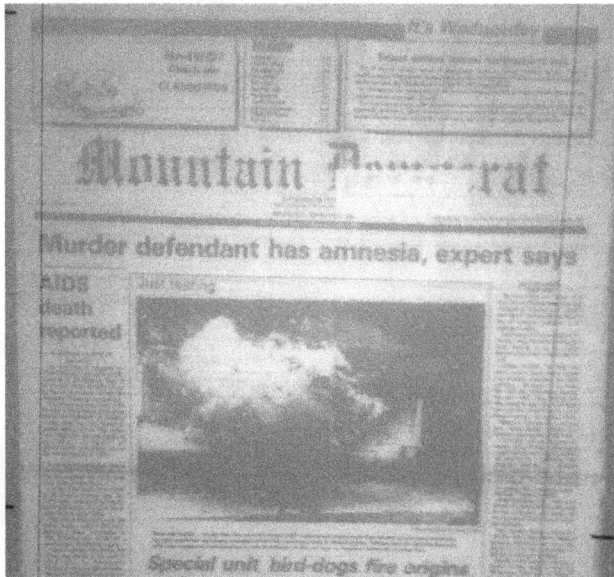

Colleen Batten forgot she was a murderess.
(Lloyd Billingsley photo.)

El Dorado County Courthouse. Two murders, same
defendant, same lawyer, different verdicts.
(Lloyd Billingsley photo.)

Colleen Harris, a.k.a Colleen Batten, a.k.a Grandma Cokey, in costume.
(Photo courtesy of Pamela Stirling. Used by permission.)

After 30 years with the U.S. Forest Service,
Bob Harris retires in 1997.
(photo courtesy of Pamela Stirling)

Colleen, Bob Harris and Sheriff Jeff Neves at
Bob's 2007 STAR graduation.
(Photo courtesy of Pamela Stirling, used by permission)

Bob Harris twice umpired the Little League World Series.
(photo courtesy of Pamela Stirling. Used by permission)

Pamela Stirling and "Grandpa Big Bear" with
grandchildren Danica, Quinn and Cole.
(Photo courtesy of Pamela Stirling. Used by permission)

"She will tell the truth."

The People of California versus Colleen Harris would play out in Department 2 of the El Dorado County Courthouse, the same courtroom as the Winkler case, and with the same judge, Kenneth Melikian. The defendant Colleen Harris arrived in a pale pink blazer tied at the waist with an oversized bow, a throwback to her first trial. In this garment, worn over a black turtleneck, the defendant appeared to be a character from a colorized movie. The CBS legal expert could have verified that Miss Colleen Harris was indeed a small and slight woman, what Pat Lakey in 1986 had called "petite." But like the dark paneling of the courtroom, Colleen was showing her age, and the pale, lined face behind the glasses hardly evoked delicacy. In this courtroom, everyone would be getting face time with the defendant.

On the witness stand she would directly face the gallery, whose left side, from her point of view, jostled with friends and relatives of Robert Harris. They included Bob's children Andy Harris, Scott Harris, and Pamela Stirling, the Los Angeles detective and mother of three who got the news of her father's violent death on the morning of January 7, 2013.

Pam was accompanied by husband Phil Stirling, a deputy district attorney in Los Angeles. The victim's sister Nancy Glaiberman took a place in the gallery every day of the trial. So did three of Bob's close umpire friends, Randy Parker, Bill Carter, and Jerry Westfall. Two of Bob Harris' female co-workers from the STAR program in El Dorado County were also regulars. Some friends of Jim Batten also showed up, though

Fred Deberry, who had testified in 1986, had since passed away. So had Jim's sister Eileen, his brother Gordon and Freida's brother Gary, with whom he had been close.

On the other side of the gallery sat Colleen's daughters Tawnie Black and Debbie Munro, sometimes joined by brother Wesley. In the earlier trial he testified as Wes Batten and was still using the Batten surname when his mother married Bob Harris. He now called himself Wesley Thornberry but did not talk to reporters about the change, and prosecutors did not ask. As Colleen had revealed to the Harris family, Wesley was the result of a one-night affair with a neighbor, Owen Thornberry. That was why the obituaries of Larry Dodge failed to mention a son. Colleen kept the truth from Wesley until he was about 40.

Wesley Thornberry was now married to Ono Batkhuu, founder of the Mongol Ecology Center, the woman he met through Bob Harris, and like Bob he had become a passionate defender of the region. In 2014 he promoted a "Ride for the Rangers" to provide new Yamaha motorcycles to the rangers of Ulaan Taiga State Specially Protected Areas. In a promotional internet video for a rally to save Lake Hovsgol, Wesley and friends showcased a cheerleading session, complete with uniforms and pom-poms. None of that flair for performance was evident in court appearances, when Wesley showed up in a dark suit. Ono was not present.

Several of Colleen's longstanding friends sat in the gallery every day. Journalists crowded into the back row, which they shared with a woman who had purchased the house in which Jim Batten had been killed, and some locals who had been around in 1986. So when Miss Colleen Harris testified, she spoke directly to people who knew what she knew, when she knew it, and in some cases whether what she said was true or false. But as in 1986, she had on her side David Weiner, elegantly dressed, still with a full head of hair, and looking much younger than his 73 years.

The defense attorney did not make a customary opening statement but said he intended to put Colleen Harris on the stand.

"She will tell the truth," Weiner told reporters. "When she tells us, you will know what happened."

In this case, Weiner would not be facing Lisette Suder, who had bested him in the Winkler case. For the prosecution of Colleen Harris, the people selected Deputy District Attorney Joe Alexander, who earned his law degree at UC Davis and had worked for the El Dorado District Attorney's Office since 2001. He had prosecuted many cases of violent crime and homicide, including the case of David Zanon, who had murdered California Highway Patrol Officer Scott Russell by running him over during a car chase. A jury found Zanon guilty and in 2010 he drew a death sentence, which he awaits with hundreds of others in San Quentin's Condemned Unit, also known as death row.

Joe Alexander had been named Prosecutor of the Year in 2013, but there was another reason he may have proved unsettling to the defendant. Alexander stood approximately six-foot-five, about the stature of Colleen's first husband Larry. The prosecutor cut a striking figure in the courtroom, where he had been placed on the same side as the jury.

"You will reach only one conclusion," he told jurors, "that this woman shot and killed her husband, Bob Harris. She shot and killed him because she loved him."

Alexander read a statement in which Colleen told Bob's daughter Pamela Stirling, "Between you and me, as I sit here wondering who I am married to, your dad just called his Mongolia love about 10 minutes ago." A day later, Alexander said, Colleen had killed Bob Harris with a 12-gauge shotgun blast at close range from just behind his left ear, causing massive damage to the face and leaving blood spatter on the ceiling.

The prosecutor called crime scene investigators who testified that Colleen Harris used Windex in an attempt to clean the blood spatter. Alexander introduced phone records that Colleen drove to San Francisco to stash Bob Harris' phone, pistol and coin collection at her son Wesley's residence. The court heard a recording of her call to AAA for assistance from Davis the afternoon of January 6. The prosecution presented cell tower readings suggesting Colleen had ditched her phone near Mount Aukum in El Dorado County. And he told the court that shortly before 3 p.m. Colleen Harris called her attorney, David Weiner. He, in turn called the police about 6 p.m. to report that a man had been killed.

"There is something else you need to know," Alexander said. It wasn't the first time she had done that.

The defense had argued that the 1986 case had "zero" relevance, but Judge Melikian ruled that prosecutors could introduce the circumstances of that case. From her familiar seat beside David Weiner, Colleen Harris listened as Alexander charted the 1986 trial.

Walter Miller had argued that Batten shot her husband, James Batten with a .410 shotgun as he was reading a newspaper in bed. She finished him off with a second round at close range, then planted a pistol on the bed to make it appear as self-defense.

"In each case, she kills her husband in the bedroom," Alexander said. "In each case, she uses a shotgun. In each case, she is going through marital difficulties. In each case, she delays reporting the crime," and "In each case she claims a loss of memory as a defense."

"He was afraid that she was going to kill him."

As his first witness Alexander called Pamela Stirling, the blond LAPD detective who got word of her father's violent death in her boss's office on the morning of January 7, 2013. On the witness stand, Stirling directly faced the woman charged with killing her father.

Pam Stirling identified Colleen Harris as "my father's second wife." They had married in 1990, when Pam was 28.

"What was your relationship like with Colleen Harris, the defendant," Alexander asked, "after she married your father?"

"Very good relationship," the detective said. "We spent a lot of holidays together. We talked on the phone. We text messaged. She helped us on our house. We bought a new house, she helped do a lot of remodeling. If we needed things fixed, she was always there to help us. She was around my three children often. It was a good relationship."

Stirling charted her father's work with the U.S. Forest Service, his retirement in 1997 and involvement with the Sheriff's Team of Active Retirees, with the El Dorado County Sheriff's Department. The STAR volunteers, Stirling testified, go through a background check, get trained in crime prevention and go to neighborhood watch meetings.

"So my dad graduated from that academy in 2007 and by 2010 he was already an instructor for the STARS Program, and that was a great joy for him. He loved that."

Stirling also outlined her father's work with the Tahoe Baikal Institute, TBI. She told the court that her father had traveled to Mongolia from June to September of 2012.

In that time frame, Alexander wanted to know, "what was your relationship like with the defendant in this case Ms. Harris?"

"We maintained contact mostly via text, a little email, some phone conversations. I was up visiting my mom at one point and we met for lunch one day." Stirling clarified that this was with "my real mom," from her dad's first marriage.

"At some point in time during the summer or fall of 2012, did you become aware that the defendant learned of an affair that your dad was having in Mongolia?"

"In September, I did," Stirling said. "I received a text message from the defendant." The date of the text was September 2, 2012.

Alexander asked Stirling to identify the defendant for the record. The detective pointed her out "Sitting next to counsel, to the right of counsel wearing a pink jacket." She had chosen the same color she wore in the 1986 trial for the murder of Jim Batten.

"And is there anything significant about September second?" Alexander asked.

"September second was my dad and the defendant's anniversary, as well as mine and my husband's anniversary."

Stirling testified that the defendant had learned about the affair through her son Wesley. Alexander wanted to know the nature of the communications with Stirling after learning of the affair but before Stirling's father returned from Mongolia.

"The nature of the conversation was the defendant texting me virtually almost every day, multiple times a day with a very wide range of emotions. She started off very sad and her surprise, ranging from anger and one day she would say 'I forgive him.' The next day she was very angry, wanted to move her stuff out of Tahoe, wanted to move my dad's stuff back to Tahoe."

As the detective testified, she did this over a two-week period. In emails, "she was talking about the affair. She would also forward me emails that she sent to her son and her son's fiancée. She forwarded me emails that she sent my father. She forwarded me an email that she sent the gal that my dad had been involved with in Mongolia."

"All right," Alexander said. "And how did the defendant tell you how she figured out the name of the woman in Mongolia?"

"She somehow was able to figure out my father's passwords to his computer and went through his computer system, went through address books, did her own, what she called her own 'investigative work' and was able to identify who she was."

"It was your understanding based on your communications with the defendant that she was working hard to figure out who this other woman was?"

"Absolutely."

"Did she share with you or forward to you a letter that she said she intended to send that other woman?"

"She forwarded me that letter," Stirling said. "And, in fact, she did mail that letter to the gal," and had paid an extra $38 to make sure it was delivered in a more expedient manner. "She followed up with an email saying your dad's lover should be receiving the letter any day. He's going to be very angry about it."

Stirling had not met the Mongolian woman, Aza, but had exchanged emails with her. Communication with Mongolia was difficult, but her father said he would talk it over with his daughter when he returned.

"All right," said Alexander. "Did the defendant ever express to you frustration during that time period with not being able to communicate with your father about the affair?"

"Did she express to you that essentially your father was not responding to her emails or her questions about the affair?"

"He was not."

"And did the defendant explain to you or describe to you how that made her feel?"

"Yes," Stirling said. "I think or I know that defendant was looking for answers. You know, she wanted clarification on what was going on. Just as I think anybody would want to know what's going on, and wasn't getting those answers. And my dad was more talking business."

Alexander reviewed with the witness a series of exhibits, including emails, the letter to Aza, and numerous texts from the defendant. Detective Pamela Stirling had forwarded those to her computer. Alexander asked why she had done that.

Text messages from the defendant, "I felt were very important to save because they were very disturbing in a lot of ways because of the emotions from which the defendant was expressing, her anger going up and down. I was concerned that some day we would end up where we are today, with another murder trial."

"Objection, speculation" said David Weiner, the defendant's attorney.

"Sustained," said Judge Melikian. "Answer will be stricken."

That ruling did not prevent the line about "another murder trial" from appearing in local news stories.

Alexander then asked Stirling "what is your state of mind was as to why you decided to save these messages?"

"I thought it was important that my dad read them when he returns to show where her state of mind is. I was concerned for my father's safety."

Weiner objected but the judge overruled.

"So you said you were concerned for your father's safety based on your communications with the defendant?"

"I was," Stirling said, and she wanted to make sure the messages were preserved.

Alexander asked Stirling if she recognized Exhibit 10.

"I do," she said. "It's the very last text message I received from the defendant. I received it on January 5, 2013, somewhere between 6:00 and 8:00 p.m. sometime before my father was murdered."

The detective's use of "murdered" did not spark an objection from David Weiner.

"After this text message did you have any further communications with the defendant in this case?"

"I sent her a text message the next day along with my father with a picture of me and my daughter at a UCLA gymnastics meet, but I did not receive a response."

Alexander admitted the exhibits, without objection from Weiner, and asked Stirling to read for the jury Exhibit 10, the text messages from the defendant on Saturday, January 5, 2013.

"I'm about to read the defendant's text message to me," Stirling said.

"Says between you and me, I sit here wondering who I am married to. Your dad just called his Mongolia love about ten minutes ago. He went outside to talk with her. When he came back in, he was instantly crying – I'm sorry, instantly trying to find me and asking me what I was doing, and then talking rapidly and telling me he was trying to find a rag to put some Armor All on his Bug-Eye seats."

In the message Colleen said: "His whole being was so different, bubbly. He gave me a kiss on the cheek and then said we should watch a movie. I have said nothing but I'm just sick inside. Who is he? What is he doing? He lets me give him back rubs and neck rubs. What should I do? He trimmed the roses today and tied up the grapes. Is he planning on staying with me and sharing a life with me? I don't know for sure. He still will not talk about anything that deals with he and I. I'm at a loss right now. Should I remain quiet or should I say something?"

Stirling had responded that she was sorry and the defendant replied, "I wish I didn't love him so much." Stirling said her father was possibly calling someone else, a friend. "No, it was her," the defendant had responded, adding, "Maybe he was checking to see if she got his special necklace for Christmas that had their two birth stones intertwined and the word together forever with their names engraved."

Stirling clarified that the "bug-eye" was the Austin Healey sports car her father had restored, and that "Cokey" was her father's nickname for the defendant.

Alexander then shifted back to the time Bob Harris had returned from Mongolia. Stirling testified that he returned on September 18, stayed with her family a few days then Stirling traveled with him to Placerville on September 21.

"And when you were traveling with your father, did he have any concerns about what it would be like to see the defendant after, you know, she learned about the affair? He was traveling in Mongolia, this would be the first face-to-face meeting between your father and the defendant, was he worried about that?"

"My dad was very worried about that," Stirling testified. "He was worried because her emails were all over the place. She was angry, she was sad, he didn't know what to expect from her. He was worried for his safety. He mentioned that, 'you know, Pam, you remember the demise of her first husband. I don't know what to expect when I get there.' And we talked in great detail about our plans once we arrived at the location," clarifying that it was the 3248 Wilderness Court location where her father and Cokey had lived since 2004. The "cabin" was Bob Harris' Lake Tahoe residence.

Stirling testified that on September 21, they flew up from Los Angeles, rented a car and drove to the Wilderness Court residence.

"And when you arrived there, was the defendant at home?"

"She was."

"And what was she like? What was her demeanor?"

"Very calm, very sad, passive, quiet."

"And did she have any reaction when your father told her that he was planning on continuing on and staying in the Tahoe cabin?"

"She was not pleased."

"And how could you tell she was not pleased?"

"Because she vocalized it," Stirling said. "She asked 'why do you need to go to Tahoe? Stay here so we can talk. No reason for you to go to Tahoe.'"

"And what did your father say?"

"He was adamant he was going to Tahoe," Stirling said. "He did not want to stay there. He told her he needed some time to think and he needed some space."

"When you said space, was he referring to space from her?"

"Space away from her."

Stirling testified that, after an hour at Wilderness Court, she and her father drove up to the Lake Tahoe cabin. Alexander asked what they had found there.

"We found all of his belongings from Placerville piled in various piles in the cabin garage floor."

"And these were his belongings that had been in the Placerville house before he left for Mongolia?"

"That's correct."

"And did it appear to you that it was almost all of his stuff?"

Weiner objected, but Stirling testified that the amount of stuff was "significant." She and her father had spent hours organizing the cabin.

"We spent most of the time just talking," Stirling said.

"All right," said Alexander. And during those conversations, did your dad tell you what his plan was? What his intent was as far as where he was going to live moving forward?"

"At that point he was going to stay in Tahoe. He was changing his P.O. box and addresses and passwords and changing everything to be at Tahoe."

"And while you were with him that weekend moving him into the Tahoe house, did he express to you any concerns about his safety?"

'We talked a great deal about his safety."

"Can you tell me what his concerns were?"

"His concerns were from when he returned was that the defendant was going to do something horrible to him as she did to her second husband. He was afraid that she was going to kill him. And we talked in great detail about safety. Being that I have law enforcement background and he has STAR law enforcement background. We discussed guns, discussed securing the house. We discussed when we were at Placerville that he was not to leave her alone. If she went into a bedroom either he or I would go with her to a bedroom. I didn't want her to have any opportunity to do something or hurt either one of us. My dad was having some neck problems and he took some medication to sleep. He didn't sleep well. And he was very concerned that when he was sleeping. He was scared that when he was asleep that he wouldn't hear her if she came through the door at Tahoe, so we discussed he should get extra locks on the door."

The LAPD detective testified that her father did add the locks.

"Did you ever have any conversations with the defendant about the fact that there had been a lock added to the Tahoe cabin?"

"She brought it up, the defendant brought it up and told me that he added a lock and that she was offended that he put a lock on his door. And she commented, 'What does he think, I'm going to do something?'"

"All right," said Alexander, who shifted his questions to the subject of guns.

"During your father's career with the Forest Service, was he required to carry a firearm?"

"No," said Stirling, who had "never known my dad to carry a gun or practice with a gun." And Bob Harris was not, she said, a "gun guy."

"Did you ask him whether there were any guns in the Placerville house on Wilderness Court?"

"We talked in great detail about that when we were driving there from the airport in the rental car. I told him maybe we should call the sheriff to escort us to the house. And my dad said I don't think that's necessary. I said 'are there any guns in the house, dad, because I don't have my gun with me?' I didn't fly armed. I didn't have the gun with me. Do we need to have someone escort us? 'No, we're okay. There's no guns in the house. Cokey doesn't own any guns. There should be no reason we should worry about guns.'"

Sterling clarified that her father had also said "not to say that she couldn't get one." A gun, that is.

"So the concern was very much there that she would do something, but he wasn't sure she had a gun. It was very uncertain. We knew she was capable of killing somebody. She's done it before."

"Objection," said David Weiner.

The court sustained the objection.

In further testimony, Stirling said she had visited the Wilderness Court house many times, never saw guns in the house, and the defendant never mentioned any guns. Her father had owned a revolver he kept at the Lake Tahoe cabin, but it had gone missing seven years earlier.

"Okay," said Alexander. "Now, while you were helping your dad settle in at the Tahoe cabin, did at any point in time did your father and you go back to Placerville?"

"We did."

"Why?"

"We went back the following morning, or maybe lunch time, because my dad was very concerned about a coin collection he had. It was a very special coin collection to him, sentimental. He bought coins wherever he travelled. And he ordered books and spent, for him, large amounts of money collecting coins from all over and putting them in binders. And he would tell me this is a binder for Cole my oldest son. And this is the princess coins that are going to my daughter. And coins that were going to Gabe and Karly, his other grandchildren. And it was just special to him. A lot of coins that took years and years of collecting. It was his thing.

"So he wanted to get the coins and he also wanted to get a small car. My husband and I had given him an old MG, a '66 MG years ago and he wanted to restore it and some day give it to my oldest son. So he spent a lot of time going into this car that he remodeled and wanted to pick that up and bring it to Tahoe."

Stirling said she and her father drove to Placerville specifically to get those items.

"And when you arrived," Alexander said, "was the defendant there?"

"She was."

"And what was her demeanor on that day?"

"The same. She was very sad, just passive, just calm, you know, not like I had expected. I was expecting confrontation and questions and she was just very sweet and very loving to both me and my dad. And she cooked a dinner and we had dinner and talked mostly about my dad's trip, small talk, nothing to do with anything with their relationship, but just small talk about the kids."

"Did the subject of taking the coin collection come up?"

"Yes," the detective said.

"My dad asked where the coins were. And Colleen had said 'why do you need the coins? Why you worried about them?' I just want to take them. I feel more comfortable taking them. I don't want something to happen to them. She said 'that's silly, what do you think I'm going to sell them or do something with them?' And he says, 'I just feel more comfortable taking them.' And she, you know, expressed that there was no reason for him to feel concerned with leaving them at the Placerville house, and so ultimately he did."

Stirling testified that she and her father drove the 1966 MG back to Lake Tahoe, and she followed in the rental car. She spent the night there then left in the morning. As she drove to the airport, she called her father and asked him to add locks on the cabin.

After a break, Alexander had the witness identify two large plastic containers with the coin collection, along with the binders.

"At some point in time did Mr. Weiner call you?"

"He did," Mr. Weiner called my cell phone a couple days before my dad's funeral service, which was on the 18th of January."

"And when Mr. Weiner called you, did he tell you that he had some property of your father's?"

"He did," Stirling said. "He told me that he had a coin collection, a handgun and a phone. He said that they were my father's, and he wanted to give them to me."

"All right," said Alexander. "And when you learned this information from Mr. Weiner, what did you do?"

"Well, I immediately called the District Attorney's Office to advise them that I had been contacted by a defense attorney."

Stirling testified that she collected the items, and got the coin collection from the DA's office.

"The end of September, last week of September towards Thanksgiving, did you and your dad continue to communicate?"

"We did."

"And did you continue to communicate with the defendant about what was going on between her and your dad?"

"There was less contact in October, but we did communicate briefly via text or email, mostly text, not that often in October."

"At some point did you learn that your dad intended to move back into the Placerville house?"

"I wouldn't use the word move," Stirling said. "He indicated he was going to go stay there to take care of the defendant because she was having hip surgery, hip replacement" in the second week of November, 2012.

"He indicated that it was a temporary situation, that he wanted to be there for the defendant's surgery, that he felt it was his responsibility to help her out and make sure she was okay to be on her own and going to be able to move around, and then that he would return to Tahoe."

Stirling's father was in Placerville through Thanksgiving, and the next day Pamela, her husband, and her three children came for a visit. Several others from the Harris side of the family were also present. Alexander wanted to know what the defendant told Stirling about her feelings toward her father Bob Harris.

"She was not sure if my father was going to stay with her or if he was going to leave her. She did not know if they were going to remain married. She was very uncertain as to the status of their marriage."

"And did she tell you what her belief was about your dad's plans after she recovered? In other words, did she believe that your father was going to move back to Tahoe?"

"She believed that my father was going to move back to Tahoe and was concerned with that."

"Did she tell you why she was concerned?"

"She was concerned that if he moved back to Tahoe, that she would lose him forever because he would have the opportunity to correspond more freely and openly with his new friend in Mongolia," a reference to Aza.

"Did you see the defendant over Christmas?"

"Yes," Stirling told the jury. "She and my father drove to our house in Los Angeles." They came on December 21 and left on December 24.

Alexander asked the witness to talk about the discussions they had at that time.

"She was very angry that my father was not having any type of affection towards her. He wasn't giving her an indication that his relationship with Aza had ended. In fact, wasn't giving any information as to the status of his relationship with Aza. She was really, really upset about finding a receipt for a necklace that my dad had bought for Aza. And she was consumed with this necklace. It had really, really bothered her, and it was clear these four days that this is something that was weighing heavily on her, and it was the necklace that had something about their names being together forever. She cried a lot and was she was more angry this time."

"Okay," Alexander said. "So at Christmas you would say she was more angry than she had been at Thanksgiving?"

"Yes. At thanksgiving she was more hopeful, and at Christmas time she was getting, I would say, fed up. You know, she said he has a year to decide what he wants, and then I'm done. I could tell she was getting frustrated with the situation."

At Thanksgiving, Stirling testified, "she thought that if he was to stay in Placerville with her, that they would be able to work it out. She would be able to convince him how much she loved him, and he was the love of her life, and she would do anything. She would forgive him. She was willing to accept everything that happened, and she wants nothing more than to be with him. She thought that by him being there. In fact, she stated that she was prolonging her recovery of her hip surgery because she wanted him to stay longer. She would kind of comment 'I don't want to get better too soon, I don't want him to leave and go back to Tahoe.'"

"And by Christmas did the defendant appear as though she had recovered from the hip surgery?"

"Oh, yes, she was good."

"And by good you mean she was physically active?"

"I wouldn't say physically active. We didn't take any long walks or ride bikes or anything. She was certainly able to go up and down stairs no problem. They helped us fix a few things around the house. She sewed some drapes for my bedroom. So, I mean, she was fine."

"And at Christmas was there any discussion about how soon your father would be moving out of the Placerville house and returning to Tahoe?"

"Right after New Year's he had to return for several reasons. One, he wanted to return, and two, TBI was starting up with their weekly meetings and my dad was the executive director of TBI for the following year and they needed to train somebody new to take my dad's job. And also my dad had started seeing a church counselor and he was hoping by seeing this counselor that he would find some answers or some assistance in helping him make the separation from the defendant."

Alexander asked about the defendant's level of physical strength apart from hip surgery.

'She very petite, very tiny, as you can see. But she is incredibly strong. Stronger than I am."

Weiner objected on grounds of foundation but Judge Melikian overruled.

"She is very, very handy with mechanics. She can fix cars. She claims to have built the house that she lives in. She built a small playhouse for my kids. She has been up on the roof many times. She cleans the gutters of her roof. She does all the cutting of her wood, her firewood. Very, very strong lady."

Alexander showed the witness exhibits with samples of the defendant's handwriting. These included a journal with two dogs on the cover and a receipt for some diamond earrings at Kohl's, on which the defendant had written "for Bob's lover." The witness also identified some samples of her father's handwriting, including a card that began "Dear Cokey."

Alexander returned to questions about firearms.

"I had a telephonic conversation with the defendant," Stirling said, "at which time she was expressing how upset she is and how sad she was about my dad's affair. And she was devastated. And that if she was braver, that she would kill herself. That if she had a gun, she would shoot herself. She said she wouldn't take pills because she probably wouldn't die and end up a vegetable. She said she was afraid of the water so she wasn't going to drown herself."

The defendant twice told Stirling about the prospect of shooting herself, once in September and at Thanksgiving. "We were sitting in the TV room, she was sitting in a chair and I was next to her in the family room, living room."

Alexander asked about any other conversations about guns.

"The defendant had told a story about a time when she lived in Montana with her three children years and years prior, and she was trying to escape from one of her husbands, her first husband, I believe, and had to live in a cabin in the wilderness somewhere, and she shot animals to feed her children."

Aside from that, long before she met Bob Harris, there were no conversations about guns. Stirling had not known the defendant to drink alcohol and never saw her take medications.

"Okay," Alexander said. "I want to turn your attention to the very beginning of 2013. And I want to start with any discussions you had with your father right around New Year's. Do you remember talking to your dad or communicating with him in someway at New Year's?"

"I do," Stirling said. "We had a couple emails, one email on the second and then another email on the fourth, but also telephonic conversations."

"And did your father express to you what his plans were for the first week of the year?"

"He was going to Tahoe."

"Did he express to you that he was moving back to the cabin in Tahoe?"

"Again, I never was under the impression nor did he say he moved out of Tahoe. All of his belongings remained at Tahoe. So he mentioned that he is going back to Tahoe and to me that was his residence. I no longer associated Wilderness as his residence."

"Did he express he was no longer going to be staying with the defendant and helping her recuperate from hip surgery?"

"Yes, he did."

"So that time frame was coming to an end according to your father?"

"Absolutely."

"Did he tell you whether he had explained that to the defendant?"

"He told her he needed time to decide what he wants, and he wanted his space to be in Tahoe."

"After those conversations around New Year's, did you have any further conversations or text messages or emails with your dad?"

"I believe the last communication was the fourth that he would have received."

"And then after that email between you and your father on the fourth, did you ever talk to him again?"

"I did not."

Stirling confirmed that her last communication with the defendant was on the evening of January 5.

"When did you learn your father had been killed?" Alexander wanted to know.

"On Monday morning," she said, "the seventh."

David Weiner began his cross-examination.

"She had been involved in a murder trial."

"The loss of your father has been a very trying traumatic experience for you, right?"

"That would be an understatement, yes."

"For you and your entire family?"

"That's correct."

Stirling said her two brothers Andy and Scott were in the courtroom and that her father Bob Harris left five grandchildren. He was a bright man with an engineering degree and master's in public administration.

Weiner retraced familiar ground about Bob Harris' activities in retirement, in the church, and as a baseball umpire.

"Was he also a private person?" Weiner wanted to know.

"I would say yes."

"Once this business came up of his involvement with the female companion or friend in Mongolia, he wasn't anxious to have that information go out to friends and family and so forth, was he?"

"No, I would think not."

"That was not consistent with the image that he portrayed?"

Alexander objected and Judge Melikian sustained. As in the Batten trial, Weiner was going after a victim who could not respond for himself.

Stirling confirmed that her brothers did not know about Aza until after their father's death.

"You were close with Colleen Harris, correct?"

"I was."

"She was your mother-in-law right?"

"Yes."

"Kind of like a substitute mother-daughter relationship?"

"I didn't see it that way," Stirling said. "I have one mom and only one mom." But she did say that prior to her father's death she had a loving relationship with the defendant, with hugs and such.

Weiner asked about Thanksgiving 2012. "That's after the time that you had shared these concerns with your father that you told us about that you and he were fearful that Colleen was going to shoot him or kill him, right?"

"Yes."

"And did you feel awkward or did you feel endangered when you went to the Wilderness Way house on Thanksgiving of 2012 with your children?"

"I did not" and the detective testified she felt no danger at Christmas, either. She was "surprised" that her father brought Colleen along.

"Did you tell him you were uncomfortable with her being in your home?"

"I did tell him I was uncomfortable and surprised he was bringing her."

Weiner dialed back to September of 2012, when Bob and his daughter came to Placerville.

"And you say that he was afraid that he might get killed when he went there?"

"Yes."

"So you discussed that with him before you went to Placerville, didn't you?"

"We discussed safety before we went there."

"And you discussed that at your home before you even got on the airplane to Placerville, didn't you?"

"I discussed it with my husband and also my boss."

"Okay," Weiner said. "And so you're a law enforcement officer, right?"

"I am."

"When you were in Los Angeles, were you concerned that you could be in danger when you showed up at Wilderness Way?"

"It was certainly a possibility."

"So you armed yourself, right?"

"No."

"You were concerned that there could be guns in the house, right?"

"I was concerned of the possibility that there could be."

It emerged that Pam Stirling had never seen the gun her father said had gone missing. She had received the coin collection from the DA, but not the gun or the phone.

Weiner asked the witness if she had taken precautions to protect herself and her father before entering the house.

"I had no means to do so," the detective said. The visit was cordial, but she was still wary.

"I was concerned of the possibility of anything happening," said Stirling, who left her father and Colleen alone while she got her nails done.

"Fair to say that during that time you were gone having your nails done, you really weren't concerned about any dangers to your father being alone with her, correct?"

"That's not correct," she said. "The possibility was there."

Stirling testified that her father was not the owner of the Wilderness Court house. She was not aware that Colleen had been involved in the acquisition of the Tahoe house in 1988.

"At the time of your father's death, did your father owe Colleen a substantial amount of money on that Tahoe house?"

"Never heard that," the detective said. She testified that while taking care of Cokey after her hip surgery, he was going back and forth to Tahoe. She did not know whether her father took Cokey on those trips.

"Did your father express to you remorsefulness towards the events that had occurred and how they affected his relationship with Colleen?"

"Very much so," she said. "He felt very, very badly for hurting her. And although they had experienced a lot of problems in their marriage over the last couple years, he didn't want to hurt her. He was no longer in love with her. He didn't think that staying with her was the best thing to do, but he cared about her and certainly wanted to take care of her."

Stirling said her father did not say he was going to end the relationship and move to Mongolia. He had joked about selling everything and moving to Hawaii.

Weiner asked the witness if her father's life was not going very well.

"I think his words were more of – and it was an email – life sure does have a lot of twists. And he had mentioned that he was going to need my love and support because things were changing in his life, unexpected changes." He was uncertain about staying with Colleen or moving on to other things.

"My dad had a pretty realistic idea of his relationship with Aza. He didn't see a long-term future with Aza. He cared greatly for her, but he did not see a potential due to the age difference, the location difference. So he was a realist in realizing, 'I don't think it could ever work, Pam, but she makes me very happy and I like what we have.'"

Stirling did not share this information with Colleen.

"I also had discussions with my dad he needed to look at the big picture. I mean, he has this wife who loved him greatly for years and years, the love of her life. And then he had another situation that could or could not have any potential, but he also was not happy with Cokey. There was a lot of drama that went on with her family that we haven't touched base on that really bothered my father, and he was having a very hard time remaining in the marriage due to issues involving her family."

Weiner did not explore the issues with Cokey's family but pressed the witness about her concern for her father's safety in Colleen's company.

"By this time a whole month and some had passed and I have to withdraw a little bit and let my dad make his decisions in what he's going to do. And as I mentioned earlier, I have a husband and three kids and demanding jobs, and it was at a point where I felt like he knew best in a decision what he was going to do, if he was going to stay or if he was going to leave. The thought of him being injured never left my mind. I was always concerned for his safety."

"So did you inquire of him whether or not he felt safe around Colleen?"

"Absolutely."

"Tell us what he said?"

"He said that he is not comfortable and often sleeps with one eye open."

Weiner pressed the point.

"My dad said that he did not think she would do anything, but considering the demise of her second husband, it was always a possibility. And that concerned him."

And he had said that to his daughter "very often."

"Okay," Weiner said. "Now, this business of her prior marriage and a husband having been killed. When did you first learn about that?"

"After my father had married the defendant, I'm guessing maybe four, five years later."

"Now, at that time did you counsel your father given your background and your employment, did you counsel your father, Dad, what are you doing marrying someone who in your words murdered her ex-husband?"

"My dad and I didn't have that conversation."

"Tell us why you didn't counsel him given your background once you learned that he was marrying a murderess?"

After an objection by Alexander, the judge had the question read back.

"When I first learned about that, it was the defendant who had told me she was involved in a trial in which she killed her husband who was a very bad man, who did awful things to her daughter. And in my eyes her side of the story sounded somewhat legitimate, somewhat interesting. It bothered the heck out of me. It bothered me greatly. My husband and I had numerous conversations about it. I seem to be the only one in the whole family who didn't know about this, everybody else knew, my aunt, my mom, my brother. I did not know about it. My dad was very, very happy with the defendant during this time. So I did not approach the subject with him. Frankly, I was a little embarrassed. I questioned why my dad would marry somebody only two years after she was acquitted of murder. I had a lot of mixed emotions about it."

Stirling said the defendant had applied for the STARS program and been turned down. Weiner objected and Judge Melikian struck the testimony.

Stirling testified her father had not told her about marrying Colleen, so she did not counsel against it.

"And she was open in discussing the facts, the fact that she had been involved in a situation wherein her husband, her then husband, ended up dead?"

"She discussed that she shot and killed him," the detective said, and this discussion happened at the Tahoe cabin, five years after the marriage.

"And who else was present during that conversation?"

"My husband was there. And there was a couple times this came up, so I don't know if he was there at that time or a subsequent time."

Weiner asked about context.

"I believe we were talking about work, it could have been one of my cases or my husband's cases, and she brought it up very nonchalantly she had been involved in a murder trial."

"Then did you question her at all?"

"I didn't." She researched the case but was only able to find some articles from the *Mountain Democrat*. She did not tell the court that the transcript of the 1986 murder trial, in which Weiner represented the same defendant, had been tossed. After finding what little was available, she did not further warn her father.

Weiner then asked whether Colleen had been a model wife to her father.

"I don't necessarily say model, but I would say she was a very good wife to my dad."

Weiner and Alexander battled over a statement of Stirling to Colleen that if her own husband had pulled something as Bob had with Aza, "I would cut his balls off and dump him." Alexander called it an "offhand comment" and "more prejudicial than it is probative."

Weiner asked if Stirling's husband was there when she arrived at the Wilderness Court house after her father's death. She was there with "the police and my husband."

"You also met there the children of Colleen Batten."

This was the first mention of "Batten" in the current testimony, but it would not be the last. Weiner wanted to know what things Pam Stirling had taken.

She had removed his two sports cars and "sentimental things."

"We took every photo of my children, which was about a box full of photos from me and my husband or me and my children. I took a couple games that I used to play with my dad. And my dad gave me silverware for my wedding and I gave him the same silverware, and for some reason I took the silverware, cheap nothing from Pottery Barn. It was sentimental because it was something he used. Maybe a couple CDs that I know my dad liked. And I think a game table that we used to play cards and poker and blackjack on. That's all I can remember."

After the lunch break, Weiner probed the witness on her communications with the defendant. It emerged Bob Harris was seeing a counselor.

Weiner then shifted gears and asked: "Do you have a financial interest in the outcome of this case?"

Alexander wanted to know what the proof was.

"She filed a lawsuit for wrongful death against my client," Weiner said.

"I think that's proper," said the judge, but Weiner wanted the question restated.

"Personally I have no financial interest in it at all," Stirling said. And if you're asking, if I'm going to gain any monies from this, my dad lived a very simple life and he did not have much money at all, so that would be no."

"Did you file a lawsuit for wrongful death? Are you a plaintiff in a lawsuit for wrongful death against Ms. Harris?"

"My family is, yes."

"Are you one of the named plaintiffs?"

"I am," she said. "Our family filed it in hopes of gaining what belonged to my father that he would want us to have. . . However, I think because of what happened to my father, what a horrible thing it was, I would not like to see anything go to your defendant."

"Anything to go to my defendant, by that do you mean anything that belonged to your father?"

"Correct."

The court ruled she didn't have to answer what that might be, and that was the end of Weiner's questions. He had left unexplored the more interesting question of whether his client stood to benefit financially from the death of Robert Harris, just as she did from the death of Jim Batten.

In Alexander's redirect it emerged that the material Stirling sought to recover was not what the defendant had dumped at Tahoe but what remained at Placerville. Stirling also said that as a STAR volunteer, her father did not carry a gun. When Stirling learned that Colleen had been a defendant in a previous murder trial, she and her father were "very happily married."

"Was your level of concern for your father's safety always the same throughout the time period of September second all the way until you learned he had been killed?"

"No, not at all," Stirling said. "It varied. Of course, it was much stronger at the beginning when I was receiving numerous text messages and emails from the defendant, in which at some point she was very angry at my father and sometimes she was very sad and forgiving, so she was all over the map. And at that point my level of concern was high, and not knowing what to expect upon first seeing her after all this time and her learning of this and receiving these various emails, my concern was very high.

"And I think there were times when it was lowered because she was so desirous of the relationship working, and she was so forgiving that I thought, okay, you know, maybe I overreacted, I didn't need to be so concerned, she seems really like she wants it to work. And maybe I just was, you know, a little more concerned based on her past and what I know from the past that maybe I was over concerned for it. But there were different levels definitely."

Alexander drew messages from the defendant that included: "I guess your dad fooled all of us living a double life and doing it so well," Stirling read. "I loved him too deeply and got totally used. I'm floating in a daze." And "All his lies and games are over with. I'm so hurt now I will make his life miserable. Your dad sent me an email and I lost it and laid everything out there. I will forward a copy to you. I'm so sorry. I know this is breaking your heart as well." Stirling told the jury these were examples of what she was receiving.

David Weiner wanted to know home many times she said she would make his life miserable. That turned out to be once, but many times Colleen said she loved her husband.

"She also told you in one of the emails that if this can't work out, then we'll go our separate ways, didn't she?"

"I think it was more along the lines she was going to give him a year to decide what he wanted to do, and if he didn't decide, she would have to move on." Stirling had no indication the defendant had asked Bob Harris to help her recover from surgery.

Alexander retraced the defendant's emails about never divorcing Bob, and about being angry and hurt. Weiner also had more questions on the statement "I will never divorce him." Stirling said she would have to review the pages, but Weiner said it was in evidence and would speak for itself. That closed out his questions and detective Stirling stepped down.

"Maybe I shouldn't say anything else."

Alexander called Robert Sheble, who for 16 years had served with Bob Harris on the board of directors of the Tahoe Baikal Institute. The prosecutor turned attention to the first week of January in 2013, when Sheble was communicating with Bob Harris on TBI business. The witness testified that Bob was set to run the organization and head the annual support campaign in March. Sheble had set up meetings with Bob for that campaign.

"We were getting together and planned to meet at Lake Tahoe on the 10th of January, Thursday the 10th. And I was going to stay at his cabin at the lake. And we were going to, during that time, sit down and detail out the campaign and also meet with the person that was going to be paid to manage the database and manage the campaigners for the organization, and we were working on a contract for this person."

Alexander asked if Bob Harris was in good spirits leading up to January 5.

"Yes," Sheble said. "He was very engaged in the organization, and was trying very hard to make things successful so that we could rebuild and be able to rehire an executive director at some soon date after that."

Alexander asked the witness about his last communication with Bob Harris. That was an email on January 5, 2013, at 4:42 in the afternoon. In questioning by David Weiner, Sheble told the court he last met personally with Bob Harris at Jack London Square in Oakland on December 18, 2012. He was his usual upbeat self and doing his Christmas shopping. Weiner also asked about Bob and TBI.

"After his passing," Sheble told the court, "we struggled for about one more year and then disbanded the organization."

The next witness, Bruce Ledesma, had also worked with Bob Harris at TBI and knew him for five years. On Friday, January 4, 2013, Ledesma received a voicemail from Bob Harris, in which his demeanor was, "as it has always been calm, a little jovial, friendly," and he "seemed to be in a good mood." On Saturday, January 5, 2013, Ledesma exchanged emails with Bob Harris, who replied at 4.44 p.m. He said the snow must be great at Lake Tahoe and that he and Ledesma should get together.

Witness John Benjamin Gussman knew Bob Harris from TBI and the California Tahoe Conservancy, for whom the witness served as attorney. Gussman first met Bob Harris in 1991 and knew his wife Colleen, whom he saw "on quite a number of occasions over the years and spoke with her on a number of occasions."

Gussman identified the defendant and told the court that on the afternoon of September 12 of 2012 he called to find out if Bob had returned to California from abroad. Colleen Harris answered the phone.

"What did you and Colleen talk about during the phone call?"

"We had some brief, polite conversation, I don't recall any details. And then I asked her the main thing that I was calling about which was whether she knew when Bob was coming back."

"And what did she say when you asked her that?"

"She said she didn't know when he was due back or when he was coming back."

Alexander asked the witness about her demeanor during the call.

"When I asked her if she knew when he was going to be back, she said she didn't know and she sounded disturbed," and her "tone of voice was disturbed."

Alexander wanted to know if the witness had heard back from Colleen Harris, who called him back about five minutes later.

"She asked me not to tell anyone what she had said in the prior conversation," Gussman testified. "I did not tell anyone about the conversation, not before this proceeding began."

"Not until after you learned that Bob had been killed?"

"That's correct."

Alexander turned attention to Saturday, January 5, 2012. The witness testified that on that day Bob Harris had sent him three emails, the last arriving at 8:46 p.m.

"I was reading and thinking about the final email," Gussman said, "and he called right around 9 o'clock, it was within one minute of 9 o'clock. And I think I picked up, but at any rate, I spoke with him right after that for a while, more than ten minutes I think."

"What was Bob's mood during that ten-minute conversation?"

"He was very cheerful," Gussman told the court. "He was cheerful and he was upbeat. And I appreciated his cheerfulness because we had a lot of challenging work to deal with together. And it was the whole situation with our organization was somewhat difficult and I really appreciated his good cheer."

Under questioning from David Weiner, Gussman confirmed that Colleen Harris told him she didn't know when Bob Harris was returning, and that she wanted Gussman to keep it confidential. After a series of questions on TBI's troubles, Gussman was excused, but the attorney took a seat in the gallery and listened as the court played David Weiner's 911 call from January 6, 2013. As the attorney explained, there had been a homicide at 3248 Wilderness Court in Placerville.

El Dorado County Sheriff's Deputy Daryl Miller told the court he was on duty that day, and had been called to that residence due to "a report of a homicide that just occurred." He was the first to arrive, and when other officers came on the scene, they set up some lighting.

"I had a view approximately 20 yards from the residence through the kitchen window," Miller told the court. "I saw a white, female adult. She was walking around the kitchen. Then she would leave the kitchen area, go to another room, come back and this went on for some time."

"Did this person seem to be under any duress while observing from outside the residence?"

"No, sir."

"Did you see this person do anything else while she was still in the kitchen?"

"Yes, sir."

"What did you see?"

"I observed her climb up onto a countertop. And once she got onto the countertop, she was on both knees, and reached up toward the top of the cabinets and it appeared she was placing an item up there."

"And were you able to see specifically what she was holding or placing?"

"No, I couldn't tell from there. It looked like something was in her hand, though."

The lady, whom Miller subsequently identified, had emerged from the house and Miller told the court he had taken her to the detectives' building in Placerville for an interview, then to Marshall Hospital for a fit-for-custody examination and blood draw.

She was cleared for incarceration and taken to the county jail.

While observing the defendant from outside the house, Miller noticed she walked with a slight limp.

"She was wearing Ugg-type boots, and I believe some sweats," a "sweatshirt-type jacket." Miller was able to see her face but saw no injuries there. During the booking process, Miller took photos that revealed "an abrasion on her middle finger of her right hand" and it was the defendant who brought this injury to Miller's attention.

"Okay," Alexander said. "Did she explain how she believed she received this injury?"

"She didn't have any idea," Miller said. "She was unaware."

In his cross-examination Weiner proved curious about Miller's firearms training.

"You work with a gun, handguns and rifles and weapons are part of your tools of your trade, right?"

"Yes, sir," said Miller, who explained his proficiency with both rifles and shotguns. He explained that the normal trigger finger is the index finger, but that someone can fire a weapon with their middle finger.

"But it's not the normal way of handling a gun, correct?"

"Correct."

"And a mark can be left on one's finger, you know this from experience, don't you, from firing a weapon with some kind of a kick?"

"Yes."

Alexander asked Miller if he was familiar with the recoil of a 12-gauge shotgun, and whether it has a significant kick.

"It does."

"If you're not handling it correctly, can it come back and strike you?"

"Yes, sir."

"If it does, that can it happen with enough force to leave injuries?"

"Yes."

"Now, the injury that Ms. Harris brought to your attention was on the middle finger of the right hand?"

"Yes, sir."

"When you're handling a shotgun, 12-gauge shotgun that has a trigger guard, where does that trigger guard fall in your hand if you're firing it with your right index finger as Mr. Weiner asked?"

"Falls on your middle finger."

"And where would it fall on your middle finger?"

"Right around the knuckle area on the inside portion."

"Consistent with the location of the injury on the defendant's middle finger brought to your attention by the defendant as you were booking her into jail on January 6, 2013?"

"Yes, sir."

The next witness, Sheriff's deputy Michel Roberts, identified the defendant, "sitting next to defense counsel wearing a pink top." She was the "elderly, white female later identified as Colleen Harris" Roberts encountered at the Wilderness Court residence on Sunday January 6, 2013.

"Did she come over to where you were standing?"

"Yes."

"And did you ask her what was going on?"

"Yes."

"What did she say?"

"She really didn't have much to say. She indicated something along the lines of 'I can't talk about it.'"

"All right," Alexander said. "Did you ask her if someone was hurt inside the residence?"

"Yes."

"What did she tell you?"

"She eventually told me that her husband was deceased inside the house" and "nobody else was inside, nor did anybody else have access to the house."

"Did you ask her when her husband passed away?"

"Yes."

"What did she tell you?"

"She couldn't give me an exact time. She indicated it was earlier that morning, so several hours earlier prior to response."

Roberts had arrived at approximately 6:20 to 6:30 in the evening. He again asked Colleen Harris what had happened.

"She again indicated that she couldn't talk about it. So not wanting to get hurt myself responding in the house, if she could tell me how he died, whether he was shot, stabbed, fell down, anything like that."

"What did she say?"

"She said he had been shot."

"Did you ask her where the gun was that he had been shot with?"

"She said that it was on the bed laying next to her husband," Roberts told the court.

"She had trouble describing it verbally. She couldn't tell the difference between a rifle or a handgun. So I asked her whether it was long or short, and using her fingers or her hands she estimated she said the gun was about three feet long."

"Did you ask Ms. Harris if it was necessary to call an ambulance?"

"She said that she was sure her husband was dead," Roberts told the court.

"Essentially there was no need for medical attention. She said you just have to go see him, you can tell."

"Did she say whether she had done anything to cover her husband after he had been shot?"

"She said that she had covered him with a blanket, and he had not moved since she covered him."

"Did Ms. Harris describe to you what her husband looked like?"

"Oddly enough, yes, she did," Roberts told the court. "She told me that he was beautiful."

"And did you ask Ms. Harris if she shot her husband?"

"She at that point said something along the lines, 'maybe I shouldn't say anything else.'" And as she said that, the deputy testified, "She hesitated for quite sometime, several seconds, broke eye contact, looked at the ground," and it all stood out in the deputy's memory.

"It's not every day you get dispatched to a homicide that just occurred, especially to one that was so gruesome."

"All right," said Alexander. "Well, let's talk about that."

Colleen Harris told Roberts he would find her husband in the master bedroom. There Roberts found a bed in the middle of the room, "and it appeared that there was a body or a person underneath the blankets on the left side of the bed if standing at the foot of the bed."

"What did you find when you pulled back the covers?"

"I found a white male that was lying in bed obviously deceased," Roberts told the court. "Most of his face was missing. I could see up into his head. He had a large hole on the left side of his face near his ear. And there was blood and brain matter, bone, just scattered throughout the room."

"Did you see anything else on the bed?"

"I saw a pistol-grip style double-barrel shotgun which appeared to be a 12-gauge."

Roberts told the court he saw no sign of a break-in, altercation or struggle. He recalled the defendant's statement that her husband looked beautiful. "And then once I actually found what her husband looked like, it really sank in it was a very odd statement."

Roberts identified various crime scene photos and told the court how he had maintained the scene "to preserve any possible evidence" for detectives and investigators. David Weiner began his cross-examination.

"You say the bed was nice and neat, meaning it looked like somebody had made it up?"

"Yeah, all the covers were on all four corners, the blankets were all the way up to the headboard."

"And she – his body was on one side covered up?"

"Yes," Roberts said, "It appeared to me that the bed had been made."

Weiner had nothing further and that ended testimony for the day.

"A shotgun blast connected with him."

On Thursday, March 19, Alexander called Tyler Katz who had performed CSI work at 4238 Wilderness Court on January 6, 2013. Katz had seen no signs of a struggle, break-in or forced entry. He told the court he saw a laptop computer in the kitchen, and found the victim's wallet in the cabinet next to the bed. He also found jewelry, medications and other items in their normal places. Nothing had been thrown about. Katz had photographed the laundry room, with small rags and towels in the washing machine.

Witness Jeremy Funk, had been one of the first deputies to arrive at about 6 p.m. and was able to see inside the house.

"I could see inside the kitchen area," he testified, "and I saw a woman walking around inside the residence. And after watching her walk around for a while, I saw her move a chair up to the counter and climb up on the counter and place some object up above the window that I could see, I couldn't see where it was placed, but I saw her place something up above the window area and get back down."

After entering the residence, Funk looked in that area.

"There was a shelf above the window and there was several jars and mugs and things like that up on the shelf. And inside a jar, some kind of porcelain contraption, was a manila envelope, and I believe there were checkbooks that were inside the manila envelope." On the kitchen table Funk found a diary with a picture of a dog on the cover, and the journal was lying on a manila envelope.

Funk also found the shotgun and Alexander asked him to describe it for the jury.

"It was a unique shotgun. I've never seen one like it before. It was a break action where you press a release, the shotgun splits in half, a double barrel side-by-side type. It had a very short or modified stock on it, and so it had two rounds of ammunition inside the two barrels."

One round was spent and the other unfired, and Funk verified from his report that the ammunition was Winchester SuperX 27-pellet shells. Funk had also documented an empty gun case he found in the garage, along with a cleaning rod. In his cross-examination, David Weiner asked Funk where he found the gun cleaning equipment. It had been on the hood of a vehicle in the garage, but Funk had not found there a handgun holster.

Weiner was also curious about the distance to the house from Funk's vantage point. He said he was about 80 to 100 feet away, with no obstructions. He saw the women move a chair and place something above the counter, but he could not tell if the woman he was watching put checkbooks into the ceramic jug. But Funk was able to identify the woman he had seen.

"She is seated next to Mr. Weiner in a pink shirt," he told the court. And prior to seeing her through the window he had never seen her before.

Deputy Anthony Prencipe had been tasked with collecting the shotgun.

"I insured it was safe," he told the court. "I wore gloves and zip tied it into the box, and sealed it with my name." He did not notice any blood spatter on the weapon.

Detective Netashia Gallagher told the court she had taken photographs of the suspect, Colleen Harris on January 9, 2013. Alexander asked if she had seen any injuries on the suspect.

"I noticed that she had a yellow greenish bruise on her center chest in her cleavage line. And I also recall when she was undressing of her complaining of pain, and saying she didn't have that bruise a couple days prior." And the defendant had not explained how she got the injury.

"She did not tell me," Gallagher said. "I recall it was as she was pulling her shirt off she had an expression on her face and complained of pain. And then I noticed the bruise and she looked at it and stated she didn't have that a couple days prior." To Gallagher the green color made it appear a newer injury, within the last several days.

David Weiner challenged the witness' ability to judge the age of an injury. Weiner said "and the other theory, of course, is this the shotgun caused the bruise, right? Putting her on to say that is, you know, no factual basis, no foundation for that opinion. And that requires an expert to date a bruise."

Weiner wanted to strike but Judge Melikian kept Gallagher's testimony as a lay opinion.

The next witness, district attorney investigator Mike Franzen, also served as a firearms instructor. He told the court his training and 19 years of experience included handguns, rifles and shotguns, and how all those weapons may be traced.

"All right," said Alexander. "In the connection or in connection with the investigation of Colleen Harris for the murder of Bob Harris, did you run a trace on a particular weapon?"

"Yes, I did," Franzen said, "It was a Boito 12 gauge side-by-side shotgun."

Alexander produced the weapon, which looked every bit as menacing as the *lupara* shotguns Michael Corleone's bodyguards carried in *The Godfather*.

"Do you recognize this shotgun?"

"Yes. Prior to today I never actually handled it in person."

Franzen had checked the serial number that day.

"The result of the trace was that the shotgun was originally sold through the Kmart Corporation. And 1980 is when it was originally sent to Kmart from the manufacturer. Based on the age of the weapon and the unavailability of further records, the ATF wasn't able to give me any transferee information after the initial transfer to Kmart." That had been in the Bay Area city of San Pablo, Franzen said.

"Can you describe any unique characteristics it has for the jury?"

"It appears to have been altered from the original configuration. The butt stock has been shortened to almost nothing. It's practically just a pistol grip at this point. It also appears that the barrels have been cut down from the original length. Just based on the cuts of the barrels, it's a very clean straight cut, and there also is no bead sight present on the shotgun.

Typically when shotgun barrels are cut down, the sight is the first thing to go because you're cutting off the front of the barrel."

Alexander asked about the craftsmanship of the alterations.

"You know, when people saw off a shotgun butt stock, they don't really care what it looks like. This one, whoever did it, actually took the time to put a recoil pad back on the end of the butt stock. Although you wouldn't really be able to shoulder this long gun in the configuration it's in, it looks like somebody wanted to make it look nice."

"A moment ago you described that this gun based on the length of the stock, you said it would be difficult to shoulder and fire," Alexander said. "Why does that matter?"

"When a shotgun is fired, for lack of a better word, there's a lot of kick. It's going to recoil to the rear with some force. And typically the reason why you do have a longer stock on a shotgun, is you are going to bring it up into your shoulder, and that helps to absorb the recoil when the weapon is fired. When a weapon is configured in the way this one is now, it only has a pistol grip on it. You would not want to bring this up in front of your face or body. You don't have the ability to absorb that recoil, so what's behind is going to get hit."

Franzen said that with the 19-inch barrel, one inch beyond legal, the recoil would be stronger. With the shells found in the shotgun, the pellets would travel at 1325 feet per second after they left the barrel, and that would equate to 2,090 foot pounds of pressure at about three feet past the end of the barrel.

"It's a strong load," Franzen said. "That is actually higher than the double-ought buck that we actually shoot in law enforcement. But 2,090 foot pounds is a pretty big number."

"All right," Alexander said. "Now, if a person was holding this gun out in front of them, would it be difficult to control the recoil such as they wouldn't get struck?"

"I think you have to have pretty substantial upper body strength to control that, and even that you're probably going to get hit."

"Would it be a degree of force large enough to cause injury?'

"Definitely, yes."

"Bruising?"

"Yes."

David Weiner pursued the recoil issue.

"If that weapon were fired with that kind of round in it from that gun, that would be substantial pressure coming back on an individual?"

Franzen said that would be so anywhere on the body, and it could cause injuries.

"If that kickback – if that weapon, butt of that weapon placed against a slender female's chest bone just covered with skin, what would you expect to see there in a couple two, three days?"

"If it didn't break a bone, I would expect there be some bruising," Franzen said, and the bruising would not be immediately visible. The coloration would also change.

"The reason for shortening the stock and the barrel is what?" Weiner said. "Normally what is someone looking for that's doing that to a shotgun?"

Franzen said it was to make them more concealable, and possibly quicker to use. But there was something else.

"When you shorten the barrel on a shotgun, it also effects the spread of the shot coming out," Franzen agreed that the shorter gun would cause more damage at close range, but there was still more to it.

"The closer you are with a shorter barrel, the more likely you are to hit what you are pointing out."

Patrol deputy Cameron Jones had been the lead crime scene investigator in the case. He told the court how he had processed the scene and Alexander asked him to describe the interior layout of the Wilderness Court House.

"As you walk in the front door, there's a living room area, a large open area directly to the left. Between the living room area and kitchen there's a small built-in bar.

There's a kitchen on the left, and then a formal dining room on the right. There's a hallway that goes down the center. As you continue down the hallway on the right side the first room is a bedroom, the second room is an office. On the opposite side there's, I believe, two bathrooms, or a bathroom and a laundry room, and a master bedroom at the end of the house with an attached master bathroom. There's also a garage that's attached that you would access through the office."

Jones told the court that in the bedroom, the shotgun was "the first thing we saw when we walked in." And it had been modified.

Alexander asked Jones if he was familiar with the term "blowback."

"Blowback is experienced when a shot is fired into a substance and the concussive force of the blast and gases leaving the firearm cause whatever the round impacts to come backwards."

"And when we're talking about a round fired into a human being and we're talking about blowback, we are talking about the blood and tissue that would spray back towards the person shooting?"

"Yes, and sometimes that would also include bone."

Alexander and the witness explored the difference between contact wounds and non-contact wounds, when the gun is not held up against the victim.

"So is there a difference between the amount of blowback you would expect depending on how far the end of the barrel is from the object being shot?"

"Specifically with a shotgun, yes, but the projectile fired would also affect that," said Jones, who agreed that shotguns cause more blowback than other weapons. He had checked the shotgun for signs of blowback but "as I recall the weapon was fairly clean."

"Did you look at the victim?" said Alexander. "Did you form an opinion as to how he received his injuries?"

"It appeared that a shotgun blast connected with him below the left ear and exited the front of his face."

"Where would the shotgun have been when it fired the round that killed Mr. Harris?"

"If you're laying in the bed, it would have been on the left corner area of the room," said Jones, who could not tell if it was a contact wound because the amount of blood.

Jones had removed the bedding layer by layer until the victim was revealed. He found the right arm behind his head, tucked under the pillow and the left arm at his side, still covered. Based on Jones' observations of the scene, the trajectory of the round would have been from what's on the right side of the exhibit towards the foot of the bed, traveling up at an angle towards the headboard.

"In the upper corner of the headboard above the clock," Jones told the court, "there's a section of the drawers, and above those drawers continues all the way up and there were indentions in the wood where pellets had made contact and actually struck the wood at that area."

Jones found no blowback on the hands or arms, as in cases where people kill themselves.

"It was not consistent with a self-inflicted gunshot wound," Jones told the court, and he found no evidence the body had been moved since the shot was fired.

Alexander asked about blood spatter.

"Close to the headboard there was the significant amount of spatter. And the further away you went, the amount of human material that was deposited on the walls and ceiling got less. It looks like it was concentrated in that area, but it was throughout the majority of the bedroom."

"And did you find anything to the right side of the bed?"

"Yes," Jones told the court. "We found what appeared to be pieces of skull. It was definitely pieces of bone on the floor, and I believe there were also some small silver pieces of metal that we assumed at the time were spent rounds from the shotgun or spent pellets from the shotgun."

"Now, when someone is shot with a shotgun inside a closed room such as the case here, do you typically find blood, tissue, bone, body parts throughout the entirety of the room?"

"Yes."

"Did you find some on the ceiling?"

"There was significant amounts of blood spatter," Jones told the court. "Specifically with the area that was above near where the decedent was, above the headboard area it appeared that it had been wiped at some point with something. The small particles of blood and matter there would have dried quicker due to their size. The larger spots appeared to have been wiped, and they would have been wet with the drying time because a larger mass of blood or human matter takes longer to dry than the smaller ones."

"What was it about the appearance of the blood on the ceiling that made it appear as though it had been wiped?"

"Small particles that were dry were still dark red in appearance and in place. The other larger, it was almost like a water stain, where what should have been there looked like it was moved and it was almost a smear mark next to it, but it was significantly lighter in color."

"So it appeared to you as though some of the blood was smeared as though someone had wiped it with a cloth?"

"It looked like someone had attempted to clean up, but very, very little time was spent on it."

"You were at the scene, you processed the scene," said Alexander. "You're familiar with all the material that was in the room. Would this be something that someone could actually clean up successfully?"

"No," said Jones, who had told the grand jury such a task would have been "almost impossible."

Alexander asked Jones what he had used to heighten the ability to see blood spatter.

"After the scene has been processed, we have a product called New Star or Blue Star, and you can spray that onto any surface. And when the lights are turned off, after a certain amount of time, the Blue Star will cause a chemical reaction with the blood and it will cause it to basically illuminate in a florescent blue color."

Jones told the court that when they sprayed Blue Star on the ceiling, he found signs of a streaking motion in one area, two to three feet square.

In his cross-examination, David Weiner asked about items that did or did not have blood spatter, a towel, a cloth, a pellet gun and a knife. Then he focused on the gun case in the garage. Jones said it was for a revolver, but he did not find a gun that fit the case. The cleaning rod had a large brush more suitable for a shotgun.

After the noon break Hillary Bantrup of the California Department of Justice told the court she had taken a blood sample from defendant Colleen Harris and found no alcohol. Angela Stroman, a firearms expert from the California Department of Justice Bureau of Forensic Services then took the stand. Stroman told the court that the shotgun in the case was a Boito model BR2, 12-gauge shotgun, serial number 30-51817A. She found that it functioned correctly, and that the trigger pull for both barrels was approximately seven pounds, the normal range for a shotgun.

Patricia McCume of the California Department of Justice told the court she was unable to find latent fingerprints on items from the scene including a wooden gun case, a Derringer, a .22 caliber revolver, a plastic Windex bottle, a cleaning rod for a firearm, and two 12-gauge shotgun shells, one spent and the other intact. McCume was also unable to find latent prints on the Boito shotgun.

Lisa Langford, of the California Department of Justice told the court she specialized in DNA and biology. She had examined the shells, the Derringer, the revolver and ammunition and the cleaning rod. None of the items yielded DNA sufficient for examination but the checkered front grip of the shotgun, and the area near the trigger, yielded DNA from the victim, Bob Harris. Langford found DNA from two other contributors but not enough to examine.

Langford had also examined boots and clothing from the defendant, Colleen Harris, a pair of black leggings, a black T-shirt with ruching, a beige bra, a white pair of underwear, and a gray and white heavy-duty coat. She found no blood on any of the items.

Alexander wanted to know, "what are the different ways in which DNA might be removed from an object?"

"You can just wipe it away, use a cloth. You can use chemicals to wipe it away. It's pretty easy, if you touch something and wipe it away, you would expect the DNA to be gone."

Langford had tested the Windex bottle from the crime scene and found DNA from the same contributors as the shotgun. One contributor was Bob Harris and the others too low to examine.

David Weiner had the shotgun brought in and asked Langford to point out the areas where she had found DNA from Bob Harris and two others. The witness would not handle the weapon without gloves.

"I ask that you hold that up and point it that way, if you will."

Langford showed some hesitation.

"It's unloaded and safe," the bailiff said.

Langford confirmed she had found no blood on the weapon but confirmed that DNA can be transferred from someone gripping the weapon. Alexander asked if it was possible for one person to transfer another person's DNA to an object.

"Yes," she said. "Secondary transfer." But Langford could not tell if the DNA in the checkered area of the shotgun came from blood or something else.

A medical emergency demanded the attention of detective Mike Lensing, the next witness, so Judge Melikian told the court they were done for the day.

"Instantaneous death."

On Tuesday, March 24, Mike Lensing told the court he had arrived at the Wilderness Court crime scene at 6:30 on January 6, 2013. Alexander asked him to describe for the jury what he saw in the bedroom

"When I entered the bedroom, it was a large bedroom, bed centered in the middle of the room, large wooden headboard with mirror behind it, and decedent laying underneath covers on the bed. Then I could see a partial butt of a shotgun sticking out from underneath the blankets. And it was obvious that the decedent had received a large wound to the head that had caused a significant amount of bleeding."

Lensing saw the dark blanket on top of the bed, but found no blood spatter. Lensing did find blood spatter on the checkered blanket underneath, and that it had not transferred to the brown blanket on top. This indicated, Lensing told the court, "that it had been placed there after the blood had either fully dried or partially dried."

The checkered blanket underneath showed small pieces of tissue and high velocity blood spatter meaning that "the source of blood had met a significant force that caused it to essentially vaporize into small pieces and exit the head."

Lensing had observed the victim with his right arm under the pillow and his head "laying to the right as if in a position of rest or sleep." Based on his observation the shotgun blast would have cause "instantaneous death" and Lensing saw no evidence the body had been moved "once the fatal shot was made."

128

Lensing told the court he found no signs of a struggle or fight but he did examine the wound.

"On the left side of the decedent's face, I saw a large area of what's called tattooing. That's where hot gunpowder comes out of the end of the barrel and causes burns on the area around the face. If that was a contact wound, you would not have that tattooing, you would have burning in a smaller area where the entry, which is generally the size of the barrel of the weapon. And in this aspect you can see where the wound is much larger, and the tattooing around the wound indicates that the barrel was a distance away from the decedent when it was fired."

Lensing told the court "the entrance wound was on the left portion of the face just at the bottom portion of the decedent's left ear, upper portion of the jaw." The position of the shotgun," Lensing said, "was down at the left leg of the decedent upside down, a substantial distance from where his arm would have been able to reach" and thus "out of place for a possible suicide." Likewise, Lensing found no blood or blowback on the shotgun, which was inconsistent with contact wounds from a suicide attempt. And bank cards, checkbooks, money, prescription drugs, televisions and such were all in place, so Lensing ruled out a robbery or home invasion.

He had also noted that "directly above and to the side of decedent's head on the ceiling was an area of blood spatter. Within that large area of blood spatter you could see some voids where there were swipe marks on the ceiling as if someone had tried to clean the blood from the ceiling."

Alexander asked what would cause such wipe marks.

"The wipe marks on the ceiling seemed to have been done a short time after the fatal incident occurred because it had started when the blood was partially dried. It had been wiped. There were areas of small swipes. You could see where droplets that were larger that were still possibly wet had been smeared." Lensing also found that "when the shot was fired, the multicolored blanket was the top blanket due to the fact that the even spray of high-velocity blood spatter." The left arm had a drop of blood of undetermined origin, but was "void of any blood spatter" the detective would have expected had the arm been exposed for the fatal shot.

Alexander directed the witness back to the shotgun.

"The shotgun did not appear to have any blood spatter," Lensing told the court.

"There was no blowback on it. It did not look as if it even had fingerprints on it. It was a very well cared for gun. It looked as if someone had taken care of it, oiled it regularly. It did not look as if it had been involved in a fatal incident like this." Lensing found "no blood smears on it. It was obvious that the shot to the decedent was fairly close. It was not a contact wound, but that whole area was covered in back spatter, tissue, high-velocity blood spatter, I would have expected to see some sort of blood spatter on the weapon if it had been used."

"Do you have any other explanation for why it was so clean?"

"That it was wiped down," Lensing said. "That it was cleaned afterward. Void of any fingerprints, void of any blood."

Lensing also told the court, "the shotgun had been placed onto dry high-velocity blood spatter. There was no transfer of the blood spatter on the blanket to the gun, so that would indicate that the gun was placed in its position we found it after the high-velocity blood spatter had dried."

"And what, if anything, does that indicate to you?"

"That indicates that some person placed that weapon there after it had dried, which is also a contraindication of suicide." Lensing told the court, "my opinion was that it was a homicide."

Lensing identified photos of items found in the house, including a cell phone registered to Robert Harris. Alexander asked how the detective obtained that item.

"We were contacted by Mr. Weiner, he stated he had some property that belonged to Mr. Harris, and he would like to release those items to us. Those items were a coin collection, handgun and a cell phone." Mr. Weiner, Lensing said, did not explain how he had obtained the items. The handgun was a Rossi model 14, .22 caliber, with ammunition in the cylinder.

"Were you ever able to recover the defendant's cell phone during the course of your investigation?"

"No, I was not."

After the break Alexander focused on the detectives' recorded interview with the defendant. At the time, Lensing and his partner Paul Hadjes did not have the defendant's cell phone or land line records, and they had not read the journal or examined the contents of the manila envelope. Neither had they listened to David Weiner's 911 call reporting a homicide. The detectives were also unaware of any information about the victim having an affair with a woman overseas.

"How about any information about the defendant having been a defendant on a prior homicide where she was accused of shooting a former husband?"

"No," Lensing said. "I did not have that information at the beginning of the interview."

In the clips played for the jury, the defendant said her last memory was on January fifth, when she and her husband had dinner and a very nice evening. She had been in a "gray fog" and her next memory was standing at the bedside of her husband. She noticed he was bleeding, that there was a shotgun on the bed, and didn't think anything of the blood because her husband normally had nosebleeds. Then she placed the blanket over the top of him.

"Her next memory," Lensing said, "is when our deputy contacted her at her house."

When detectives asked her whether she killed her husband, she stated that she loved him and would never do that. She said the shotgun was a gift from her husband, from the decedent because she had been raped in her home several times. And he had gotten that so she could protect herself when he was away. Lensing had told the grand jury he had found no evidence for the rape claims, and presented no such evidence in court that day.

In the interview the defendant claimed she did not know her husband was dead. And as the detectives told the grand jury she was joking around at times and never asked questions as to why she was being interviewed.

During the interview, Lensing learned that the defendant had been involved in a prior homicide case, but he did not know that she had made an amnesia claim in that case. Lensing told the court, "I'm trying to her to get her to talk to me about what happened. She is just claiming she just doesn't know." Lensing said "I had no indication it was an accident at that time."

The detectives asked whether the defendant knew any local attorneys because they had learned David Weiner, present in court that day with his pink-clad client, had in fact called in the homicide.

After the break, before they played the rest of the tape, Alexander brought in witness Tom Kulesa, a nurse at Marshall Hospital. He testified that in January of 2013 he had attended to a woman who identified herself as Colleen A. Batten, and identified her in court as the defendant. Kulesa told the court she brought no injuries to his attention and did not complain of pain.

Marshall's emergency room doctor, Roger Gallant, identified the defendant then viewed records of his fit-for-incarceration exam for "Colleen Batten." She denied any headache or chest pain but said she had borderline high blood pressure, osteoarthritis and fibrocystic breast disease and Lyme disease. Gallant said that the defendant had no difficulty recounting her medical history and fully understood all his questions.

"And did you see," Alexander said, "any sign she was suffering from, or did she complain to you that she was suffering from, a loss of memory or recent loss of consciousness or awareness or anything of that nature?"

"No."

"Did she report she was suffering from amnesia?"

"She did not."

"Okay," said Alexander. "Is loss of memory something that would be fairly significant in your evaluation of her that evening?"

"Absolutely," said Gallant, who told the court he would have documented such a claim and followed up with more testing. The defendant, he said, did not appear anxious but did show flat effect, an unemotional, fatigued response to questions.

"Now, did you attribute that flat affect to anything in particular?"

"Well," Gallant told the court, "the report was that there had been a recent death in her family to her spouse, and so I attributed some of that to that."

In his questions for Gallant, David Weiner referred to "Ms. Batten Harris," a clear attempt to link the cases.

"You did not find from your examination that she appeared to be under the affect of any kind of anxiety reaction grief reaction or altered mental status?"

"That's correct," Gallant said, and in his physical examination did not see the chest bruise. Weiner showed him pictures of the injury. If the photographs were taken on January 9 and 10 of 2013, he wanted to know, would it be out of the realm of possibility that that bruise was caused on January 6 or 7?

"I would say it would not be out of the realm of possibility, no." And Gallant did find her fit for incarceration.

Detective Lensing returned and Alexander noted the end of the interview, when detective Hadjes had asked the defendant whether her husband was having an affair or seeing someone, a woman in another country.

"That was the most engaged, little that she was, during that time. During this time she seemed to have a little bit more energy and was able to articulate better."

"Did she ever indicate any difficulty remembering details when you were talking about this subject matter?"

"No."

Lensing told the court he had returned to the Wilderness Court residence for an additional search on January 9.

"That search was in reference to a possible hiding spot that I was told about where there could have been a spot in an attic items could have been hidden," Lensing said. "The attic access was inside the bedroom, the same room where decedent Harris was in. When I was at the attic access, I looked to my right, I noticed on top of the bed stand there's the bed and then there's two cabinets on either side of the bed. At the top of that cabinet was a Windex bottle."

"Did you notice anything about it when you retrieved it from the top of the headboard?"

"Yes, the top of the headboard was filled with dust, but the Windex bottle had no dust on it." And this was the same Windex bottle they had discussed earlier.

"Now, on the ninth did you also attempt to interview the defendant's son Wesley Thornberry?"

"Yes."

"Was he willing to talk to you?"

"No, he was not," Lensing said. "He had not had a chance to speak with his mother's attorney, and that he stated that once he did that, that he would be willing to talk to us."

Lensing told the court he had also located keys to safety deposit boxes associated with Ms. Harris. He secured a warrant and on January 28 examined the boxes, at two separate banks but found that Wesley Thornberry had been there first, on January 8, the date confirmed by the banks' surveillance video.

Lensing also obtained phone records for the victim, the defendant and her son Wesley Thornberry.

"When you reviewed the records for the defendant's cell phone, did you note anything?"

"Yes," Lensing told the court. "I noted that during the period of time that she had stated that she had amnesia, sometime from the evening before until, what, 24 hours later we contacted her, she stated she didn't know what happened. Well, in the morning I found out that her cell phone had placed several calls from several different locations between Placerville and San Francisco."

"During the day of Sunday the sixth?"

"Yes," Lensing said. "There were two phone calls to Triple A," the road assistance company, and those calls had been made at 12:24 and 12:34, both from the same location. They played the calls in court, and the jury heard the voice of Colleen Harris, in full control of her faculties and without any sign of amnesia.

Alexander put up a chart and had Lensing walk through a timeline of January 6, based on the phone records. The first call came at 7:26 a.m. off the tower at Missouri Flat Road near Placerville, and it was the defendant's call to her son Wesley. She called him again at 7:48 from a location near Folsom. Next came the defendant's 9:15 call to Wesley in San Francisco, then another at 9:41. At 12:08 p.m. the defendant received a text from daughter Tawnie Black, which came in from a tower in Vacaville, followed by the Triple A calls at 12:24 and 12:34, the second cancelling the request for service. The last activity was a call or an error message at 3:19 p.m. that pinged off a tower in Mt. Aukum, near the defendant's house. None of the calls had been recorded and detectives had not recovered her cell phone.

Alexander turned Lensing's attention to the landline, which the defendant had used to call David Weiner at his home at 2:51. The call lasted six minutes and 50 seconds and no other calls emerged from that line that day.

At 6:05 in the evening of January 6, 2013, David Weiner called 911 to report a homicide at the Wilderness Court house. At 6:46 the Sheriff's department called that residence.

"During your interview with the defendant," Alexander asked Lensing, "was she able to give you her cell phone number?"

"No, she wasn't."

"Did she tell you where it was?"

"No, she could not tell me where it was."

In his cross-examination, Weiner asked Lensing, "when you refer to the murder of Mr. Harris, that's what we're here to decide, isn't it?"

"That's correct."

"You used that term 'murder' in response to counsel's questions a number of times?"

"I don't remember if I did or not."

Lensing confirmed that Wesley Thornberry and his mother had access to the safety deposit boxes. Weiner was not entirely happy with the detectives' diagrams of the crime scene, particularly the position of the shotgun.

"Until death do we part."

On March 25, a brisk Wednesday, Weiner continued his cross-examination of detective sergeant Mike Lensing.

"Can you tell us what size bed that was, like a Cal king or queen or regular king?"

"I don't know," said Lensing.

Weiner reviewed the entry wound on the left side of the neck just under the left ear and "the general path of travel of that discharge was from that point off through the face next to the nose on the other side of the face."

"Yes," said Lensing. "I believe it would be the right cheek."

Weiner then focused on the ceiling, which Lensing said was the standard eight feet. With the bed at a couple of feet, that would leave about five and a half feet above the body.

"And the blood spatter was directly above the head or off to the left or right or, what, if you can tell us?"

"The blood spatter seemed to be centered over this area, the main portion. With some pieces in various portions of the ceiling all around."

"Pieces of flesh hanging from the ceiling?"

"Yes."

"Small fragments?"

"Yes."

"Can you explain to us why there would be debris above the head in a perpendicular direction, approximately a perpendicular direction as to where the shot was fired through the head?"

"Yes," Lensing said. "As from what I'm understanding the other expert had testified there's a lot of pressure involved with a shotgun blast. And the head of the human body contains a lot of fluid in there. And when that skull is broken and a lot of gases are introduced to that head, it bursts, and a lot of pressure and a lot of fluid come out, and that's the reason for the high-velocity blood spatter all around the bed, the spatter on the ceiling, and the parts of blood and tissue throughout the room."

Weiner engaged the witness on the difference between blood spatter and blowback. Lensing said that blowback has less force. Most of the shotgun pellets had been recovered, but he did not have an exact count.

"Was there any stippling on the tissue near the entry wound, correct?"

"Yes."

"And that stippling is from the burning of the powder in the flesh?"

"Yes."

Weiner asked Lensing to estimate the distance from the muzzle of the shotgun to the victim. The detective declined to guess. "I can't even estimate," he said. "I don't have the basic data." And he had not checked the barrels of the weapon to see if one was clean and the other dirty from being fired.

Weiner then shifted to his client's "flat affect" during the interview.

"In the questioning session with Mrs. Harris, you said people block things out because they have been in a traumatic situation. Do you recall that?"

Lensing did not but Weiner read what he had said from the transcript.

"Okay. And, you know, accidents can happen. People block things out because they are traumatic, and I realize that you love your husband dearly, and you never want to hurt him."

"Were you lying to her when you said that?" Weiner asked.

"No, I wasn't lying to her," said the detective, explaining that he had been trying to elicit a respond to his questions.

"You know from experience and your own personal knowledge that people block things out because they are traumatic, correct?"

"I have heard that yes."

In his redirect, Alexander asked if the detective was "also aware that people can claim they don't remember something to avoid responsibility?"

"Yes."

"How common is it for a criminal defendant or a criminal suspect to lie or claim a lack of memory in your experience as a law enforcement officer?"

"More times than not you get people that lie to you in some shape or fashion initially."

"Looking at the gunshot wound," said Alexander, "do you have an opinion as to whether the wound could have been inflicted by a .22-caliber revolver?"

"No, it could not," said Lensing adding even with "snake shot," a cartridge with small pellets, the .22 could not have inflicted that damage. Snake shot had also been eliminated in the case of Jim Batten, struck twice with lethal blasts from a .410 shotgun.

The detective also discounted the antique Derringer as the murder weapon. As for the defendant's "flat effect," that had changed at the end of the interview when detective Hadjes, brought up the issue of whether the victim was having an affair.

"Yes," Lensing said. "That was the first time during the entire interview that I actually saw her perk up a little bit, sit up in her chair a little more, and actually engage in conversation with us. And the level of her voice was higher than what it had been in the prior interview or in the prior part of the interview."

Alexander then called Kenneth Barber, a sheriff's deputy who had been on the scene at Wilderness court and recovered a diary on the kitchen counter. Barber recognized the journal and Alexander had him read for the jury a passage from September 5, 2012.

"How do I begin and end this final chapter in my journals. I never felt so empty so destroyed, my life core completely draining from me. A year of torture. Mongolia. A 35-year old teacher. A year-long affair. One sentence shared with me. I can't wait to feel your naked body next to mine again. All the sneaking. So many lies. Thankful to this new love of his life."

The pink-clad defendant was looking toward the deputy as he read, making it difficult for those in the gallery to view her response. Alexander directed Barber to read another portion.

"And then you call me, 6:30 a.m. on September second, our 22nd anniversary and tell me you drove quite a ways from the camp to find a signal so you could call me on this special day of ours to wish me a happy anniversary and tell me how much you loved me. I was so happy. It had been so long since you had said these words. I was crying when I got off the phone. And then Wes said 'what did Bob say?' When I told him, he then said, 'is that all he said?' The look on his face and tone of his voice immediately told me something was wrong. He got tears in his eyes and said we would talk later. I forced him, begged him to please tell me. Oh, my God. Why would you call me and do this? And then have an entirely different life going on. How could you do this?"

Alexander asked Barber to read yet another portion.

"Were you hoping I would get angry or get a divorce or maybe kill myself then your image would not be destroyed? Sorry I couldn't fulfill your plans. I just am hopelessly in love with you and always will be. I am destroyed beyond belief. I have managed to recover so many times over the years from so many and have many scars, but this time I am so deeply destroyed I don't even know where to begin. You are my prince, my everything."

The time frame for the entries was Sunday, September 9, 2012. Barber read another:

"This has hurt me so deeply that I will probably never stop believing and I will never let another man near me. I am so empty, so numb right now. I hope my daughters' new partners never hurt them like this. If I had a gun, I would blow my head off right now and end this torture and nightmare I'm going through right now. I let him get to my core and now he has destroyed me. Oh, God."

Barber read other entries in the same vein, and one that indicated Bob was coming home.

"My husband, the love of my life, the man I no longer know who he is, finally came back from Mongolia 9/18/12, and stayed three days with Pam before the two of them arrived here. Since that time he is living at Tahoe still Skyping his 35-year old lover and has informed me he's going to continue to do so and continue helping her financially and pay her rent. Geez, he's so different from a year ago, very secretive, very closed, very distant. I'm trying so hard to get some kind of affection from him. It's painfully slow. How this girl got so much from him in one year amazes me. She is one smart girl. There's no way she loves him but somehow her

139

sex and attention have wrapped Bob completely around her and makes him happy and will do anything for her diamond earrings, trips, money, food, birthday gifts, etcetera. Where do I fit in, his wife of 22 years? And he tells me I'm the perfect wife and always have been, yet I'm the one being punished and the one he will no longer be affectionate with or want to be with. This is so unfair. I don't understand. He has gone to the priest."

In a November entry the defendant wrote:

"It is now November and I will soon be having surgery and Bob has said he will come down from Tahoe and take care of me, as I was there for him through four surgeries. Maybe we can continue with life together and move on from this girl. I hope so. I truly love Bob and want to share the rest of my life with him, but I won't accept this girl as part of the package. Only time will tell. She is not giving up easily but I will never divorce Bob. I made a promise to him and God I would be by his side in sickness and in health, for better or for worse, to love and to cherish until death do we part."

The long entry ended:

"I'm dying inside. I don't know what to do. I am so lost right now. I'm going to confront him and get some answers. What is he doing? Why is he continuing? He said it's not about me, yet I'm the one being punished. Why? He gets so angry when I try to discuss this, but I can't go on like this. He needs to talk. His image means everything to him. He was so angry I told Pam."

That closed out the readings from the defendant's journal, but few in the court were prepared for what they heard next. Alexander told the court he was going to take the unusual step of reading David Weiner's testimony, a stipulation to which they had agreed.

"My name is David Weiner," Alexander read. "I am a criminal defense attorney. I represent the defendant in this case, Colleen Harris. If called to testify I would state the following under oath: One, I previously represented the defendant, Colleen Harris, in 1985 when she was arrested and charged with the murder of her husband James 'Jim' Batten. At that time Colleen Harris was named Colleen Batten. Colleen was found not guilty in that case.

"Two, my relationship with Colleen Harris has always been

professional in nature. Colleen and Jim Batten did some surveying work for me prior to 1985. After the trial in 1985, Colleen briefly worked for me as a paralegal. In January of 2013, I lived in Plymouth, California."

The testimony included his home and office telephone numbers at the time.

"On Sunday afternoon, January 6, 2013," Alexander continued. "I received a telephone call at my home in Plymouth, California, from Colleen Harris. After receiving that call I showered, dressed and drove to Colleen Harris's house located at 3248 Wilderness Court in Placerville, California. I met Colleen Harris at 3248 Wilderness Court on Sunday afternoon, January 6, 2013. Colleen and I spoke for approximately one and a half hours, 90 minutes. At no time did I enter the house. Colleen Harris did not give anything to me, and I did not give anything to Colleen Harris. I did not see or hear or otherwise become aware of anyone else being at the house while I was there. Colleen Harris was dressed in clean, casual clothing. I did not see any blood on Colleen Harris, and I did not see any injuries on Colleen Harris.

"After meeting with Colleen Harris, I drove from 3248 Wilderness Court to my office in Cameron Park. The drive took approximately 35 minutes. From my office I called 9-1-1 to report a homicide had occurred. I have reviewed People's Exhibit 21 and agree that it is a true and accurate recording of the 9-1-1 call I made on January 6, 2013. Although I placed the call to 9-1-1 from my office in Cameron Park, California, for some reason it was initially routed through my home phone and the first 9-1-1 operator to answer was Amador County dispatch.

"After calling 9-1-1, I called Colleen Harris's home phone. I also called Colleen Harris's son Wesley Thornberry. I spoke with Wesley Thornberry on the phone during the evening of January 6, 2013. I told Mr. Thornberry his mother had been arrested and asked him to come to Placerville, California. On a later date on one or more occasions, I met with Mr. Thornberry, both at my office and my home. On one or more of these occasions Mr. Thornberry gave me the following items: a cell phone, a coin collection, and a .22 caliber snub-nosed handgun. I later turned these items over to law enforcement.

"At this time I do not recall the exact date when I received these items nor whether I received them from Mr. Thornberry at my home or while at my office. I agree that People's Exhibit 17 is the cell phone. People's Exhibits 48 and 49 are true and accurate photos of the coin collection. And People's Exhibit 14 is the .22 caliber snub-nosed handgun. All three of these exhibits are the items in the same or substantially same condition as when I received them from Mr. Thornberry. I am aware that Mr. Thornberry has stated that there was a handwritten note he believed to be written by his mother Colleen Harris attached to these items. I do not have that note nor did I ever have that note."

As the jury heard, David Weiner clearly recalled that Colleen Batten had been found not guilty for the 1985 murder of Jim Batten. On the other hand, the attorney could not recall the more recent date when he received certain items, such as the victim's gun, phone and coin collection.

Alexander thanked Weiner then called Rich Horn, another El Dorado County sheriff's deputy. Horn told the court that on January 15th of 2013, he was tasked retrieve a firearm at the residence of David Wiener, who told the deputy it belonged to the Harrises. Horn found it loaded, except for one cylinder. Horn traced the serial number and found that Bob Harris had purchased it in 1972 while living in Redding.

Heather Spohn, a criminalist with the Western States Information Network, had made a graphic display of Colleen Harris' cell and landline calls. Alexander traced it for the jury. On January 5, 2013, there were 19 text messages sent and received on that date, all off a tower near her Wilderness Court residence. Spohn gave the times of the messages and who they were from. The last landline call went to John Gussman, Bob Harris' colleague at TBI.

Spohn covered the Sunday, January 6, 2013 calls to and from Colleen Harris in great detail, from Placerville to San Francisco and back, showing the last pinging off the tower at Mount Aukum. Wesley Thornberry's cell activity that day ended with a brief 5:59 p.m. call from David Weiner. The location of Colleen Harris' cell phone remained a mystery.

Alexander called Dr. Gregory Reiber, the forensic pathologist who had performed the autopsy on Robert Harris. Reiber told the court he had earned his medical degree in 1981 and practiced forensic pathology for 29 years, performing more than 9,500 autopsies. Reiber told the jury how he conducts an external and internal examination, and outlined the difference between contact and non-contact wounds. Like Dr. Robert Anthony, the pathologist in defendant's 1986 trial, Dr. Reiber showed considerable familiarity with shotguns.

Alexander asked Reiber what caused the death of Robert Harris.

"His cause of death was a shotgun wound of the head," he said. "The wound on the outside of the body, the diameter was large. It was about an inch, which is typical for a shotgun entrance wound. It was about an inch, which is typical for a shotgun entrance wound. Secondly, there were shot pellets recovered from the body internally along the path of the wound. And there was a piece of wadding consistent with material from a shot shell recovered from inside the head."

Reiber told the court the entrance wound was directly below the left ear. The exit wound "appeared to involve the area of the mouth and nose with some additional separate pellets exiting through the right cheek. The wound was noncontact and Reiber categorized it as "a close-range wound."

Alexander wanted the jury to know how close the shooter had held the muzzle from Robert Harris when the shot was fired.

"My best estimate is three to six inches, perhaps as far as a foot, but I doubt that it was even that far. I would say three to six inches is the most likely range." The exit wound "really encompassed this entire area, center of the face, the nose was partially separated from the rest of the face and flapped over to the right." And Reiber found seven wounds from separate pellets, which had collided with each other in what he called a "billiard ball effect." Reiber found "soot and searing" and also stippling, indicating that the wound was close range.

"The wound track basically went to the right and from back to front through the lower part of his head. The left side of the mandible, that's the lower jaw, was very much fractured. Much of the upper jaw was also fractured, which would be underlying this area. The skin was torn at the edges of this exit wound up into the right upper eyelid. A lot of that is tearing, not probably directly exit wound. Many of the teeth were loose. The tongue was badly injured. The lower portion of the skull was penetrated by multiple pellets. And there was wadding both in the area of the nasal cavity and up in the lower part of the, what we call the cranial cavity where the brain is. Most of the pellets came out of the mouth and nose area. Again, a few out the right cheek and a few penetrated into the cranial cavity and grazed through the lower portion of the brain."

When Bob Harris was killed, Reiber told the court, "the shotgun would have to be positioned out to his left, the muzzle within a few inches of this point on his head, lower head, and you'd have to have the barrel, the trigger action and all that and whatever stock there was out in this direction and not down against the pillow, but up at least somewhat above the pillow."

The entrance wound, Reiber testified, was "a location that's very atypical for a self-inflicted wound." Something on the back side of the head, he said, is "very unusual for a self-inflicted wound" and the wound track also inconsistent with a self-inflicted wound.

"It's a close-range wound and it's at a very odd angle. It would require an individual to use both hands to hold the weapon," Dr. Reiber said. "The hands would have to be holding the weapon out to the left, aiming it somewhat toward the front of the head so you would have to have one hand steadying the barrel at a few inches from the skin, the other hand around the action, if you will, of the weapon, with probably a thumb on the trigger."

The victim's hands, Reiber testified, were in an unusual position for anything like that to have taken place. The blood spatter was also inconsistent with a self-inflicted wound but Reiber was not surprised to find it on the ceiling.

"That would be very typical, in fact, for a shotgun wound of the head," he told the court. "So with shotgun wounds to the head you typically have a large debris field in terms of tissue and blood debris around the location of the head."

Alexander asked if the position of the body and the wound track were consistent with someone standing next to the bed, leaning forward and firing at Mr. Harris as he laid sleeping.

"Yes, it would," said Reiber, who told the court he had seen nothing inconsistent with that view.

Alexander had the bailiff bring in the sawed-off 12-gauge double-barreled shotgun for Dr. Reiber to handle and observe.

"It's definitely muzzle heavy," Reiber told the court. "My first observation it would be extremely difficult to control with one hand, which would definitely confirm that you would have to have two hands if you were going to shoot yourself at a less than contact range, you would have to use two hands. Now, if you turned it upside down, now it's still very muzzle heavy. It would be very hard to control. And to actually make sure you were aiming it at yourself, I would expect the other end to be braced with a hand or braced against the body."

Reiber demonstrated with the weapon.

"Holding it away, it moves all over the place. If I was in an emotional state to shoot myself, it would probably be even harder to keep it steady. It doesn't have any balance because the stock, the stock is almost completely gone, so there's no counterbalance to it, that's one of the reasons it's so muzzle heavy."

Alexander asked Reiber if there was anything about this firearm that would cause him to change his that this is a gunshot wound inflicted by another.

"No," he said.

Alexander retrieved the weapon and Weiner began his cross-examination. The attorney was curious about the positioning of the body when Reiber received it, but the pathologist said it was consistent with the crime scene photos.

"Can you tell us by pointing your finger to the right side of your face where the center of that wound was on Mr. Harris's face?"

"Yes," Reiber said. "I would put the center of the exit wound right here in the middle."

As in the 1985 proceedings, Weiner pursued questions on the time of death.

"It's really hard to pinpoint," Reiber told the court. "For rigor to reach its maximum, which it appeared to be pretty much in his case, it takes roughly 12 hours at typical indoor room temperature."

Weiner asked Dr. Reiber about bruises, and if their color changes over time.

"Oh, yes," the witness said. "The first color change tends to be the color gets more dull that originally especially with bright pink bruises turn to a dull pink. If you have a purple bruise it will turn more of a dull purple. The next color change is the edge of the bruise starts to have a little bit of brown color to them. The next color change you see is from brown to green at the edges."

Weiner showed him photos of the defendant's chest bruise and asked him to estimate the time. "How about within three days, doctor, possible?"

"Possible, yes," Reiber told the court.

In his redirect, Alexander called attention to the same photos. Reiber agreed that the bruise would be consistent with the person firing a shotgun and having it hit her in the chest. Then he called attention to the small injury on the right hand.

"It's the kind of injury that you sometimes see when a firearm is fired using the right hand not securely held enough, and actually the trigger guard itself slides in the hand and that can actually injury both the index and middle finger and perhaps even the thumb depending on how the weapon was held."

Alexander asked if being struck in the chest would trigger a dissociative state.

"I wouldn't expect so," Reiber said.

If a person fainted from such an injury, Alexander asked, and were aroused, "would they have a 24-hour period where they claim they remember some things and not other things?"

"On the basis of this injury, no, I would not expect anything like that," he said.

"That would be the kind of thing you would get from an actual concussion, what we call traumatic brain injury." The doctor added that "even with a concussion, I would not expect amnesia going forward from the event. Perhaps going back for a short time, but not forward."

Reiber told the court he had not changed his position that Bob Harris had been resting or sleeping when shot at a slightly downward angle.

"Do you know, Doctor," Weiner asked, "if someone's memory can be temporarily discombobulated because of extreme trauma, something that effects one psychologically?"

Alexander objected and Dr. Reiber said he would defer to a psychiatrist or psychologist. On the other hand, the forensic pathologist had shown the court he knew all about shotguns, and what happens when someone fires one into a person's head at close range.

Judge Melikian told the court the next witness, Wesley Thornberry, Colleen Harris' son, was on his honeymoon and unavailable. The court would play a DVD of his testimony from May 28, 2014.

"*Things were a little crazy.*"

On March 26, an unseasonably warm day in the foothills, Wesley Thornberry was not present in court but he would still testify in a video that on January 6, 2013, he missed a call from his mother but got a text stating: "Need to talk to you. Coming down." Such a message, he told David Weiner, was not unusual. Thornberry also explained that Weiner called to tell him his mother had been arrested. He drank some wine and went to bed, and on Monday January 7 drove to Placerville to meet Weiner. There, and in nearby Cameron Park, he accessed a storage facility and safety deposit box on behalf of his mother. These contained documents, envelopes, silver coins and jewelry. He gave all this to Weiner, who had power of attorney on the Cameron Park facility, an arrangement Colleen Harris had requested after her arrest. Thornberry alone had access to the box in Placerville, where Wesley stayed until his mother's first court appearance.

Joe Alexander asked Wesley why he brought the collection to Weiner and not to law enforcement.

"David seemed the best person," Thornberry said. "Things were a little crazy. It seemed like best decision. I can't explain it now." A note with the material said to give this to Pam, Bob's daughter from a previous marriage that also produced Andy and Scott. Wesley said he knew them and they were friendly. But Pam Stirling, listening attentively from the gallery, knew nothing of any such note.

Under questioning from Alexander, Wesley could not recall telling

Weiner what he knew about the coin collection. He had been "running ragged" those first two weeks. He did say he found "more stuff," including a brown bag with a pistol, which he did not recognize. He also brought this pistol to Mr. Weiner. He said he was not familiar with guns, but knew this was a revolver and assumed it came from his mother's place.

Wesley Thornberry also testified that he had not visited his mother in jail, because he "didn't want to see her in that environment." And he had not talked to her or written to her, explaining that he "didn't want to."

Colleen Harris was facing the video screen, so those in the gallery were not able to assess her response. But at all times her profile was clearly visible to the jury on her right and Judge Melikian on her left.

In the taped testimony, Thornberry noted that his maternal grandfather Irwin Eugene Yates owned a liquor store on Cutting Boulevard in Richmond. He had been robbed and owned guns, which Wesley saw as a child. On the tape he was presented with people's exhibits 10 and 11, of a double-barreled shotgun. Thornberry said he "never saw that before."

Judge Melikian handled an issue with a juror then said the court would hear an "audio exhibit," an eight-minute tape of the 911 call from July 27, 1985. Melikian told the jury they couldn't use the material to conclude that the defendant was "disposed to crime or of bad character." Members of the jury had been issued transcripts of the call.

"What's the problem?" said dispatcher Lynn Wheaton.

"I think I shot my husband," Mrs. Batten said.

"Were you having an argument?"

"Uh, yes, I think. I don't know. I don't remember anything. I don't know if I even shot him."

"Is he there in the house with you?"

"Uh, I think so."

"Does he need an ambulance?"

"I don't think so."

The dispatcher could not find Wilderness Way on their maps, so they ask for directions.

"1200 feet past Hank's Exchange, heading east," Batten said. "You take a right and its, stay on the paved part of road, third house on the paved part. It's a large three-story shake house, with a big 20 by 30 deck in the front and there's some lights on the outside, I think."

"Can you tell me where the gun is?"

The response was inaudible. Mrs. Batten did say that here husband was "on the floor" in the bedroom, and that she was in the living room.

"Oh God," Mrs. Batten said. "He's lying on the floor. He won't get up."

The dispatcher asked if they had argued recently.

"It was today," she said. "He told me he was going to shoot me if I didn't. . . He told me he was going to shoot me."

Colleen Harris sat motionless during the playback of her own words, the second time she had heard them in a courtroom. Then she heard another familiar voice, as Joe Alexander called Dennis Theis, the sheriff's deputy who had responded to the 1985 call, and who still worked part time for the department.

"A woman had called and said she shot her husband," Theis said. The officers had gone to the front door, where Mrs. Batten let them in. Deputy William Crutchley asked Mrs. Batten if she was the one who shot husband.

"I must have shot him," she said.

The officers asked about the body, which was upstairs, but as to the location of the gun, "She doesn't know," Theis said. Asked what happened, "She said he threatened to kill her." Theis duly advised Mrs. Batten of her rights and listened as she hugged a pillow on the couch and spoke spontaneously, not in response to questions.

"Is he dead? I must have shot him. Did I shoot him?" She also said that her husband "raped my daughter, Tawnie" since she was 12, and she was now 21. Her husband hated the kids especially Debbie, whom he reportedly described as a "contentious bitch." She asked him for a divorce but he said he would kill her first. Theis quoted her as saying: "I want to die. I love him so much. I must be crazy." She told the officer she built the house, built everything and "He told me I had to leave."

Theis told the court Mrs. Batten was talking into a pillow, so the sound quality on his tape was poor. He reviewed it when he wrote his report the next day. He told the court they found Mr. Batten in an upstairs bedroom "lying on floor between bed and wall, on right side, in large pool of blood," and that he was "obviously deceased."

Theis told David Weiner, then and now Mrs. Batten's attorney, that they found a revolver lying on the bed but did not collect evidence. The deceased had a "large one-inch hole on left side below arm and waist. Also a hole the same size on his right side in the chest." These wounds were made by a "shot-firing weapon" and the officers saw pellets on the bed and floor.

Mrs. Batten "held her hand over her mouth" when talking to the police. She was crying off and on and "seemed, in mental stupor of sorts." On the other hand, Theis said, "at times she appeared very lucid." And the officer told the court that the statement "Is he dead?" is "not a normal response to the question whether she shot her husband." Those words seemed to linger in the courtroom.

Officers Crutchley and White had since passed away but Dr. Robert Anthony, the forensic pathologist who had performed the autopsy on Jim Batten, was still active in California. In the September 6, 1985, preliminary hearing, still available in transcript, Anthony had testified about the wounds from the .410 shotgun that had destroyed Jim Batten's lungs and heart. In response to questions from David Weiner, Dr. Anthony had shown familiarity with all varieties of shotguns, including a 12-gauge, but none of that testimony was recalled and Dr. Anthony did not appear.

What witnesses had said in the 1986 jury trial could be easily established with a transcript of those proceedings, but since the trial ended in acquittal that transcript had been tossed. So instead of the actual record, the court heard testimony from Pat Lakey, the journalist who covered the earlier trial for the *Mountain Democrat*, as she said, "gavel to gavel." She told the court the Battens were going through a divorce, each serving papers on the other. They were living in separate homes, she said, 250 feet apart, "out near Hank's Exchange, between Diamond Springs and Pleasant Valley."

As Lakey described it, when Colleen went to his home to discuss the divorce, he became angry, held a gun to her head and demanded a sexual act while he taunted her about her daughter. He "forced her to perform oral copulation" and told her that her daughter enjoyed that. Mrs. Batten "heard the gun click, thought she was going to die." After that it was a "blank spot in memory" until her father called "asking if Jim was all right." As it happened, Lakey's memory also had some blank spots. The journalist could not remember, for example, whether Mrs. Batten had called her attorney before calling 911. The still available transcript of the preliminary hearing confirmed that Colleen Batten had indeed called David Weiner before she called 911.

Lakey also noted that psychiatrist Dr. Norman Tresser had testified, but did not recast any of his testimony about "psychogenic amnesia." Under further questioning from Weiner, the journalist could not remember the kind of gun involved in the shooting of Mr. Batten. That too was readily available in the preliminary hearing transcript, and the single-shot .410 shotgun had been one of the exhibits in the jury trial Lakey covered gavel to gavel.

On the subject of oral sex, Lakey said Jim Batten told his wife she "didn't do it as well as her daughter." And according to Mrs. Harris, her husband "could be violent at times." He was "very kind but could snap at a moment's notice and become violent."

All this was based on a single journalist's recollection of what the current defendant had said in court nearly 30 years earlier. Mr. Batten had not been on trial then, was not on trial now, and no longer available to respond. As in 1986, the district attorney had not called Freida Batten, who in 14 years had never seen a trace of abuse from the man. In 2015, nearly 30 years after his death, the last document she possessed from their relationship was the letter from the Boy Scout leader to the Colonel at Stead Air Force base, praising Jim Batten for his "conduct beyond reproach."

Batten's friend Michael Bowker, Pat Lakey's colleague at the *Mountain Democrat* in 1986, also knew a thing or two about Mr. Batten and his marriage to Colleen. He was still in California and readily available but never called to testify.

Like Jim Batten, Robert Harris, was not available to testify on his own behalf.

Still, the jury had plenty to ponder, and would get more on April 1, after a break for the Cesar Chavez holiday.

"Homicide? Suicide? Or murder?"

On April 1, defense attorney David Weiner had reserved seats for his client's family, and the gallery was packed solid. As before, the victim's relatives sat on the other side, rather in the style of the British parliament. An El Dorado County murder trial left little room for bipartisanship. No television cameras were present, but one news photographer from the *Sacramento Bee* stationed herself in the corner.

The defendant Colleen Ann Harris entered through the front wearing black slacks and a heavy chartreuse-magenta blouse, a variation of her 1985-6 courtroom attire. Her hair, streaked with gray, swept back in a ponytail. News reports still described her as "petite" and, true to form, when seated beside her attorney, only her head and the top of her neck appeared above the back of the chair. After the five-day break the courtroom had been full at 8:30 but the proceedings did not commence for a full hour. Judge Melikian finally entered and David Weiner began his opening statement.

"You're here to make some decisions," he said, from behind a movable podium. "The prosecution said in their opening statement that Colleen Harris killed Robert Harris because he loved him. That's not true." The case, Weiner said, was "about love, betrayal and survival, in the most basic instinctive way we know." It was about people's "basic instinct to protect themselves."

Robert Harris was "a good man, an educated man, a talented man." Weiner explained how Harris met Colleen when he was 15 and she was

13 on California's north central coast. His parents were camping out and her parents were staying at a lodge. She saw them fishing in the Eel River and "walked down in her nice dress and patent leather shoes."

That day she learned how to fish, Weiner said, and caught three or four trout. Robert and Colleen "became friends" and they connected later, when he was 16 and she was 14. She was shy, but they went out to a movie. When they met again many years later, Robert had earned an engineering degree and a master's in public administration. By then Robert had married.

Weiner told the jury Colleen had entered a nursing program in Montana, where she learned how to hunt and fish. There she met and married Larry Dodge, a PhD candidate at Brown University. The marriage "ended in abuse," with Colleen "escaping with her children and leaving Mr. Dodge" in New York.

Back to Montana, she "had nothing," and lived in a cabin with her three children. "She survived," Weiner said and "learned how to use guns very well." She shot small game and elk, "with a 30/30." So "she knows how to place the butt of a gun to protect herself."

As Weiner brokered the story, Colleen and the children returned to California, to Lake of the Pines, where her father owned a lodge. There she lived with the children and, after inheriting money from her mother, she got involved in real estate. This led her to hire local surveyor James Batten, and that story, Weiner said, was "an important part of this case." James Batten "was killed in 1985" and a jury found his wife not guilty.

Batten had been good with the children and "they loved him." Weiner pointed out the children in the courtroom. Debbie, he said, was a professor of engineering at Portland State University. Tawnie is a paralegal and Wesley an executive with The Gap. Back in the day, Weiner said, the kids wanted her to marry Jim Batten. Colleen learned surveying from him and the two formed a productive business and "made a lot of money."

Around 1979 and 1980, Weiner told the court, Tawnie began having bleeding problems in her vaginal area. Dr. Rosen told Tawnie to stop having sex with her boyfriend. Trouble was, she didn't have a boyfriend. As it turned out, Weiner said, Tawnie had been molested by Batten starting when she was 11. And he threatened her if she told. When Colleen learned about the "oral sex" and "vaginal" sex, she told him "you are out of here." She got his gun, which he kept in a drawer, made sure it was unloaded "and ran him out." She went to the sheriff and brought charges. Batten left but the children wanted him back. He got counseling and the authorities dropped the charges.

"Five years go by," Weiner said, and "things were not going well." While Colleen did all the work, James was at the golf course, drinking. And he got "mean to children" and "things disintegrated." It wasn't working and "she wanted to end it." So she contacted a lawyer.

Batten had been divorced before, Weiner said, but did not reveal that Jim Batten's divorce from Freida had been amicable. Had she been called, Freida Batten could have testified at length about their relationship. In Weiner's version, Colleen approached Jim Batten with a list of the assets, which were "mostly hers," and he came back in a rage. There would be no divorce. "I'll kill you first," he supposedly said. "You're not gonna wipe me out."

Weiner told the court that in one confrontation, he held her down with his knee in her chest, put a gun to her head and forced her to perform oral sex while explaining "your daughter does this much better than you. And that never stopped." The next thing she remembers, Weiner explained, was talking to her father on the telephone while in jail.

"She doesn't remember," Weiner told the jury. "She suffers from a memory loss."

Weiner represented her in that trial and gained an acquittal. Now some 30 years later, with the same client, same charge, and in the same courthouse, he explained that she started life again, picked up the pieces and continued the business.

At one point "Robert Harris reappears," contacts Colleen and pursues her. The jury learned that Harris had one contact with Colleen when she was married to Batten. Colleen told him about the Batten matter but it proved no impediment and the two duly got married, and the union lasted 22 years. Bob Harris, Weiner explained, was the former treasurer of a Lake Tahoe organization, with the environmental MEC group in Mongolia, a member of the Knights of Columbus and an usher. He was "about image" and a private man who protected his privacy, but "Robert Harris isn't what everybody thinks he is."

He was "involved with a Mongolian girl" named Aza, and he was "leading a double life." Things aren't going well but he won't discuss divorce. He is living in Colleen's home and she functions as a caregiver, cook, housekeeper and gardener.

As Weiner explained, Bob owed Colleen about $200,000 on a Lake Tahoe house they put in Bob's name. Bob had been through a divorce and been wiped out. It wasn't going to happen again, Weiner explained. Keeping Aza and Colleen was the "best of both worlds" and Bob wanted to sell the properties and move to Hawaii, which the attorney said was "closer to Mongolia than California."

Colleen wasn't going for that and moved four truckloads of his stuff to the Lake Tahoe house. There were three guns in the house, a shotgun, a Derringer in a file cabinet, and Bob's .22 revolver, which she didn't want in the house. After James Batten's "death," Weiner told the jury, she sold all the guns.

The evening of January 5, 2013, had "special importance." Bob was in a telephone conversation with Aza, and Colleen didn't want to confront him. Still, Weiner said, "Bob flew into a rage," a change "from a bubbly personality to a completely different individual." He was holding Colleen's cell phone and screaming at her for calling his daughter Pam, which violated his "directive" not to discuss the matter. "You have betrayed me," he said and threw down phone, "enraged," while calling her "foul names." Bob evidently retreated into a room and Weiner told the jury that the present trial was about what happened there.

"Homicide? Suicide? Or murder?" said Weiner "I will leave that for her."

His client was "a passive individual," and "She doesn't remember something and she'll tell you she doesn't." But Mr. Weiner did have command of some facts.

He told the court that when his client Colleen had been in jail in 1985, her house had been burglarized. The attorney did not explain that the burglary had been discovered by Colleen Batten herself, after her release on bail and before the preliminary hearing. As the *Mountain Democrat* reported, in an article headlined "Batten home reportedly burglarized during jail stay," Colleen told police the coroner's seal was broken and a hidden key missing. The only items she reported stolen were two 241-C computers and a card-reader computer, and she provided no estimate of their value. Weiner left such details unexplored and jumped ahead to 2013.

After "Bob was dead," he told the jury, Colleen was "in an emotional state." The hours went by and she was "not knowing, not understanding, some kind of a nightmare." But she wanted to carry out "Bob's bidding," and worried about a burglary like the one in 1985. As Weiner explained, "She needed to protect Bob's coins," and his gun, which carried "sentimental value." So she took these down to her son Wesley's place in San Francisco. On the way back she "blacked out or something" and "found herself in a spinout" west of Davis. Three men stopped to help and got the car running. That was the "last time she remembers the cell phone."

Back up at the Wilderness Court residence in El Dorado County, Weiner told the jury, she was "faced with an impossible situation. Bob was clearly dead. Nothing could bring him back." So she "did her job and started cleaning." Weiner described "pieces of flesh hanging from ceiling," and his client "went up with toilet paper to clean it. She knew it was her job to make the place presentable." So she "made up the bed neat," and "adjusted him a little bit." She "put left arm on his chest" covered him with a blanket, and "calls David Weiner," her attorney from back in 1985.

"He makes arrangements to meet her outside the house," Weiner explained, and "spends substantial time with her." And the attorney told the jury that "she'll tell you about her state of mind," and "what happened when law enforcement arrived." This concerned how her "husband's face ended up in a bloody mess" and a bruise on her chest, in the "shape of the end butt of gun." His client, he said, "will explain how this occurred" and he urged the jury to "draw your own conclusions" and render his client "not guilty for the murder of Robert Harris." But he wasn't done.

He said his client had no sleep from the morning of January 5, 2013, to January 7, when officers interviewed her, a full 45 hours. One detective had stated there had been "dust on the gun" but no blood.

District Attorney Joe Alexander noted a detective's testimony that the gun had been wiped down, that there had been oil on it, and that the weapon was "well cared for."

The jury did not learn where the defendant's phone was when it pinged off the closest tower to 3248 Wilderness Court. Investigator Martha McKenney had measured various driving distances and times in Placer and El Dorado counties. She did not drive to Davis or San Francisco and rendered no information on any cell phone towers.

"You have to live-track a phone if you want to know where it is," Alexander responded. "You can't do it later."

The morning session of April 1 yielded no knowledge of the phone's whereabouts. The afternoon session began with an exchange between Weiner and Alexander over Norman Tresser, the psychiatrist from the 1985 case. According to Weiner, Dr. Tresser had suffered a stroke and could no longer testify. Alexander did not challenge that statement, but he did question the probative value of "calling an expert inferentially," and without the opportunity to cross-examine. Judge Melikian ruled that Weiner could ask the client if she sought treatment from a psychiatrist "and that's it."

Alexander did not invoke a different psychiatrist but he had not showed up empty handed. He had brought along a 14-page declaration from April 2, 2003, presented by Tawnie Black in a quest to get a restraining order against her mother. In this sworn document, Colleen says, "If you weren't such a slut, this never would have happened" in reference to the events with Mr. Batten. This was a different response, Alexander said, than the defense had portrayed. The declaration also charged that Colleen Harris said "I can fool any counselor" and scoffed at counseling itself.

In the lengthy declaration, Harris treated the daughter not as an abuse victim but "like the other woman." When Tawnie was 22 years old, James Batten was still coming on to her. Her mother said if Tawnie and Batten wanted to marry, "I'll step out of the way."

Judge Melikian wanted Alexander to "water down" the slut statement. Weiner wanted it just the way it was. The bailiff brought in the jury and Tawnie Black, now in her early 50s, took the witness stand. The resident of Battle Mountain, Nevada, told the court of her experience as a paralegal, legal secretary and administrative assistant. She was 21 when she testified in the earlier case and 10 when she met Jim Batten, the surveyor.

"He was really nice to us three kids," Black told the court in a soft slightly raspy voice. "We all just really loved him" and "begged mom to marry him." At the time they were living in a trailer park in Auburn, then moved to an apartment in El Dorado, near Placerville. That was where the trouble started, according to Tawnie Black.

She told the jury that when she was 11, Batten came in when she was taking a bath, pulled open the curtain and said "you shouldn't be ashamed of your body" but not to tell her mother. That night he came into the bedroom and put her hands on his penis. Then he came every night, and it soon became more than touching.

"He put my mouth on his penis until he ejaculated," Tawnie Black told the court. This went on for a couple of years, and then intercourse started at 13, accompanied by threats to hurt Tawnie and her mother.

"My mom is a very classy lady and raised us kids to be classy," Tawnie told the court. Her mother, facing her from directly in front, did not look at her daughter during this testimony.

Jim Batten got counseling and apologized, but then the molestation and threats continued. Tawnie told the court he even pursued her after she left home.

"Your mom and I are getting a divorce," he had said. "Now we can be together." Regarding Mr. Batten's demise, Tawnie's memory was somewhat sketchy, but she recalled the "time of his death." Her mother looked sad that day and was crying. Tawnie heard people coming to house but doesn't remember the sheriff's officers.

In his cross examination, Joe Alexander established that Jim Batten had been killed on July 27, 1985, when Tawnie was 22. Alexander asked about Colleen's attitude toward the abuse she had suffered. "At first a lot of remorse," she said, but her mother also said "hurtful things." Pressed for details, she did not elaborate.

"If you weren't such a slut, it never would have happened." Alexander said. "Did she say that?"

As Tawnie pondered her answer, she did not look at her mother, seated beside attorney Weiner.

"I think she was hurt when she said that," Tawnie said. "She looked at me like the other woman. She didn't really mean that."

Tawnie testified that her mother "told me I needed to behave myself, not to wear provocative clothing and keep my robe on." Tawnie described herself as a "shy teenager" but "I did have some tops that may have been more sheer, that may have been considered provocative."

Her mother "said she didn't think she needed counseling," Tawnie said in court. And Mr. Batten "should not have come back." Her mother had asked her what sexual positions they practiced, and if she enjoyed the sexual activity. The 2003 declaration also revealed that her mother said not to press charges. She would be "dragged through the mud on the witness stand."

Alexander asked if Tawnie's mother had ever called her a liar.

"She may have," Tawnie said.

Alexander asked if her mother had said: "I can outsmart any counselor, so that would be a waste of time and money."

"She has said that, yes," said Tawnie, who had to serve her mother with a copy of the declaration and file it in court.

Alexander asked Tawnie if she told her mother that she was interested in marrying Jim Batten.

"I don't think so," she said, but Jim was interested in marrying Tawnie, who was estranged from her mother for "a long time."

Alexander asked if Tawnie had "attempted to reconnect" with her mother. Tawnie said she did so on December 31 or January 1 of 2012, "before Bob died." Tawnie said she called him "Bobber" and "he was my step-dad."

Weiner again took up the questions. Tawnie's ex-husband didn't like her mother because she was "too controlling." But she was "going through post-partum depression" when she signed the 2003 declaration. She was "in a fog" around that time, and the ex-husband was the driving force behind the declaration.

Tawnie told the court she has been through five marriages, "embarrassingly so," and because of PTSD she "can't trust a man" and "will not get married again." But she had "not changed one bit" on her mother, who was "wonderful, loving, supporting, protecting" and "makes you believe in yourself." On the other hand, Tawnie was "stuck with the declarations I signed" but her mother, she said, did not coach her to say things about Jim Batten.

Under questioning from Joe Alexander, Tawnie said she would not say "anything" to help her mother, and that a lot of the things in that declaration had been false. Her mother had called her a slut, for example, "but not right at that moment."

Alexander also produced a handwritten declaration Tawnie had filed in March of 2003, when she was 40 years old. Alexander asked if that one was all true.

"Yes," Tawnie said.

In that declaration, the mother is not described as "wonderful." In fact, Tawnie had written that she was terrified of her mother because she saw her pull guns on family members.

Alexander asked if she had seen him pull a gun on Jim Batten. No, she said, but she had seen her mother pull a gun on Larry Dodge.

"She never protected me," Tawnie had written in the declaration. Alexander asked if that was true.

"When you go through sexual abuse you don't feel anybody understands," Tawnie said.

Under resumed questioning from David Weiner, Tawnie said the declarations were "designed to make mother look terrible" and she would "not sign them today."

She said Larry Dodge had been attacking her brother Wesley, beating him and slapping him, and that mom "used a gun" to ward him off. Weiner noted that Wesley, who had been two years old at the time, was present in court. The attorney did not note that Larry Dodge was not able to testify.

Tawnie and Deborah's actual father, Lawrence Burnham Dodge, passed away at 69 in a Dallas hospital on July 17, 2012. It would have been accurate to say that Mr. Dodge, a professor, photographer and songwriter, had in fact "died." Step-dad "Bobber" Harris, on the other hand, had been killed, gunned down in a way that plastered part of his head all over the ceiling. As Mr. Weiner said, Colleen Harris would get into all that her own self, her second one-woman show on the same courtroom stage.

"I threatened to blow his head off."

On Tuesday April 7, 2015, a storm rocked northern California, blanketing the Sierra with snow. In Placerville and below, it was all rain but traffic was moving along on Highway 50, which runs right behind the Eldorado County Courthouse on Main Street. Upstairs in Department Two, Judge Melikian thanked the jury for braving the conditions and Joe Alexander questioned "Miss" Colleen Harris, the defendant. The deputy district attorney wanted to know which phone she used to call David Weiner.

"I think I used the home phone," she said, but she "wasn't sure if she made any calls." It had been brought to her attention that she called Weiner and, she said, "Dr. Tresser helped me a lot."

Joe Alexander had posed no question about the psychiatrist from the 1986 trial, and David Weiner had told the court that Dr. Tresser had suffered a stroke and was unable to testify. Yet, the psychiatrist was fully able to counsel the defendant.

Alexander did not pursue the point and asked the defendant if she was basing her testimony on memory or on reports she had recently read. About James Batten she retained "very little memory" but did recall it as "so devastating" and said that Batten had been having an affair with the wife of a neighbor she did not name, as she told detectives after the death of Bob Harris. She was "tired and confused" and "foggy and distraught" when talking about that. The fog had again drifted into the room.

Alexander asked how the Batten and Harris cases were similar.

161

"They are not similar," the defendant said. "Why is he in the picture? That was 30 years ago."

"Would it be fair to say," Alexander said, "your memory comes and goes when you're talking about offenses you don't want to talk about?"

"At the time when I'm confronted with disaster," Miss Harris responded, "I've discovered that my mind does shut down." And at the time, "people were pointing guns at me," speakers blaring and dogs barking. So she was "totally gone."

Harris told the court she knew Bob was dead when she asked her attorney David Weiner to call 911. She went to San Francisco to make sure Bob's coins were not going to be stolen because she knew she would be in jail and the house vulnerable. Alexander posed some questions about the trip back, when she called AAA, then asked about the time she pulled a gun on Larry Dodge.

She said that had been in Montana in 1972. She grabbed Wesley and Dodge came and knocked her down. She left and returned with a gun. Dodge grabbed the daughter and said "Go ahead and shoot." Harris said she informed the police but did not have the police report. But the testimony confirmed that she had pulled a gun on Larry Dodge.

Alexander asked if she remembered pulling a gun on Jim Batten from memory or from reviewing documents. That was September 17, 1979, and she had "threatened to blow his head off." She did remember this in detail, so what she wrote in response to Tawnie's 2003 declaration, that she had never pulled a gun on anyone, was that a lie? Alexander wanted to know.

"I guess it would be a lie, yes," she said. But the quest for the restraining order was "so shocking." She told the court "I'm not trying to lie but I must have."

The defendant said, "I'm not denying that I pulled a gun" but Alexander noted that she had denying doing so, under oath.

Still under oath, she told the court Batten took his gun "all over" in his truck and at home kept it in a nightstand. Harris said he had threatened to shoot her daughter.

"I was going to get him out of the house," she said. "I threatened to blow his head off. I did." She knew he kept ammunition in the office cabinet on the second floor, and that "other guns" were in there.

Alexander recalled the click and the gap in her memory. "Do you remember how he was shot?"

"No."

The deputy district attorney asked the defendant why Jim Batten had been found with his pants on.

Harris said she had "no memory" of that. It was "based on something I read." Alexander asked what it was that she had read.

"I don't know," She said. "I had piles." But the documents talked about how he was on the floor, that there was blood on the floor, and that she had made a phone call at the other house."

Alexander pressed the point. If she had no memory after the click, how did she know Jim Batten was on the floor? This too, it turned out, had come from the reports she had read. Her memory was intact up until she heard a click, but she did not tell 911 or deputy Crutchley or deputy Theis about any sexual assault.

"That was not until the trial?" Alexander said.

"I don't remember the trial," the defendant told the court.

In further testimony Colleen Harris said it was not true that she treated the daughter like the other woman.

Alexander asked why she described Tawnie as "the daughter." And did David Weiner prepare a script for her?

"No," she said.

Alexander asked if she knew Weiner prior to Batten being killed.

"Yes," she said. Weiner had in fact defended Batten on the molestation charge.

Alexander asked if she told deputy Theis she loved Jim Batten.

"Yes, I did."

Did she tell Theis about the sexual assault?

"I might have," she said. "I don't think I did."

Harris told the court she continued to use Batten's name on legal documents. The total value of the property they owned together was $652,000.

"It all became yours," Alexander said.

"Yes."

"Where is Jim Batten buried?" the deputy DA asked.

Harris said he had been cremated and buried on the property at 4721

Wilderness Way. A plaque had been put up but the house had been sold and it was no longer there. Alexander asked what the plaque said. The defendant could not remember.

She did recall that she had no contact with Tawnie for about ten years, but the daughter reappeared around 2012. In late September of that year Colleen wrote "how do I begin and end this final chapter in my journal?" Alexander asked why she had written that.

"For myself," she said. "I did want children to know what was going on after I was gone." It was "My thoughts about life" and she was "always trying to keep in touch with who I am."

She also intended Bob to read it, but at the time she and Bob Harris were not talking, and she knew of his affair with Aza. Still, Colleen was doing all the cooking, though there were times when "he did a few things" and she was "surprised what he was capable of doing." She was doing 90 percent of the cleaning, though "once in a while he would throw his umpire stuff in the machine." She had told detectives, Alexander noted, that she hadn't been doing laundry because of hip surgery.

"I guess I said that," she said. "I don't know why."

Yes, she did all the yard work, "but he pruned roses." He also helped clean the barn and the whole house. He did this, it emerged, even though his left arm was tingling and his right arm had an elbow implant. He came over every day, she said, and moved back in before her surgery.

Alexander began to focus on Saturday, January 5, 2013. She was home alone with Bob and heard him on the phone. She saw Aza's number and "went into bathroom, so he wouldn't feel I was spying on him." He was talking to her and "I wanted to see what he was going to say."

In Colleen's account for the court, Bob said he was looking for a rag to put Armor All on the car. She went out to help him, but then they decided to watch a movie. When asked for specifics, she again mentioned Dr. Norman Tresser, and Alexander called for the judge to strike that.

They were watching the movie but became distracted. Colleen went to use the bathroom and left her phone on the couch. When she returned, a red-faced Bob was holding the phone, and "angrier than I had ever seen him in 22 years." She tried to calm him down but he slammed down the phone and shoved her into a burl coffee table.

"I was between him and the coffee table," she testified. "I don't remember falling on it but I probably did. I don't know for sure." And she wasn't thinking about any injuries from the scuffle. Bob was "super angry" and fled to a bedroom. After a time his wife Colleen followed him into that bedroom.

"What time?" said Alexander.

"It was dark," she said, "night time," but she had "no idea" of the exact time. Was it before midnight?

"Yes, I think," she said.

Again it was "pitch black" and she couldn't see anything. She described taking off all her clothes. "I was naked, yes," she said. In her account she was under the covers and talking to Bob while "giving him a neck and body massage" as she did every night. Bob, who was on his side, was stiff at first but started to relax.

"What's the next thing you remember?" Alexander asked.

"I felt something," Colleen said. It was some kind of metal, and by then she was on her knees leaning over him. The metal object was next to his body, on the right. Alexander asked if this metal object was under the covers.

"Yeah, it was under," she said. "I mean it was just, I felt the metal there. It happened so fast. I was rubbing him and I hit something metal. That's when everything just went crazy."

Alexander asked if she knew this metal object was a gun.

"It flashed into my mind," she said. "What is it? Is this a gun? Bob, what is this?"

"Get the 'F' away from me," he reportedly said, with Colleen adding, "I don't swear."

After that she said, "Why do you have? I just threw out all kinds of things. Was he trying to commit suicide? Kill me?"

"What did he say?"

Colleen Harris could not remember her conversation with Bob at that point.

Alexander asked what happened next.

"He flung me off him," she said. "I went flying off. He knocked me over on the bed. I went down. I was not on my knees any more. I felt something hit by my chest" as she was "groppeling around." She felt something hit her in the chest.

"What hit you in the chest?" said Alexander.

"I wasn't thinking," she said. "I was trying to get away from whatever it was."

The deputy district attorney asked how many times she was hit in the chest.

"Probably two," she said. "I'm trying to think if I felt it twice. Next thing I know, I must have been knocked out for a little while. I don't have any memory for a little bit."

Alexander asked if she remembered anything else prior to the time when she had no memory for a little bit.

"He was screaming and ranting, told me it was all my fault, I betrayed him." They wrestled around a little bit. As he was pushing me off he said everyone had betrayed him."

Alexander asked if the blow was significant.

"Yes," she said.

"After the blow, no memory?" he said. "Anything else that happened?"

"I was still in bed, next to him. That's all I can remember." She said "he just bodily got me over there. I had something."

"A gun in your hands?" Alexander said.

"I think that it was there, yeah." She repeated that she was "groppeling" with it, then the blow hit her "like a sledgehammer," she said, indicating the middle of her chest, adding, "I am telling you the truth."

"After the sledgehammer blow?"

"I came to, really quiet."

"The blow is the last memory?"

"Yeah," she said. Bob was still grappling with the gun, and she was "unconscious or had the wind knocked out of me. I wasn't aware of anything around me for a while."

Alexander asked what happened in the bedroom when she next became aware.

"I said, 'Bob, are you okay?'"

The sledgehammer blow did not knock her out of bed. She went to get up.

"I thought he had a nosebleed," Colleen Harris told the court.

"Had the lighting changed?"

"No," she said. "It was still pitch black, but the eyes adjust. . . I could kind of see his body. A little bit. I got up and put a blanket over him. He had been fighting a bronchial infection."

"You were able to make out what you think is a nosebleed?"

"Yeah. Then I saw the gun."

"On the bed?"

"Yes." The gun was "up close to his body" and partially uncovered and tangled up. She described covering him up with a dark blanket. Alexander asked if that was because of the bronchial infection and she was worried about him being sick.

"I started becoming concerned," she said. "I went into bathroom and put on glasses," and turned on the light. "Oh my God," she said, in a wail. "Just awful, just horrible!"

"Bob had a massive gunshot wound to the head?"

"Yeah."

"You knew Bob absolutely was dead," Alexander said. "No nosebleed?"

"I did."

Alexander asked how long she was in the bedroom before realizing Bob was dead.

"No idea," she said. It was before the sun came up though still pitch black in room. But before she turned on the light she was "able to see the gun on bed."

Judge Melikian scanned the gallery for inappropriate responses to this sensational testimony. Colleen Harris rattled on about Bob taking a lot of Tylenol and Ibuprofen. He had dental issues and his gums were bleeding and swollen. "He needed to floss" and had an appointment the next Wednesday.

Alexander asked if Bob had hit her with the gun.

"I don't know," she said.

"Did Bob let go of the gun?"

"I don't know," she said, then more about "groppeling" around and feeling the blow while "right next to Bob in bed."

Alexander asked the defendant if she had told the jury everything she could think of.

"Yeah, I think so," she said

"Are you leaving anything out?"

"At this moment, no."

When she came back to awareness, Alexander wanted to know, was she on top of the covers, or underneath the covers?

"I don't know," she said.

Alexander asked what she did after she saw Bob's condition. Harris said she was "screaming and crying," saying "This can't be. Bob, please." In a wailing voice she said "I went in this like a fog. I wandered all around. It isn't real. Tell me this isn't real."

"Did you call 911?"

"No."

"Call an ambulance?"

"No."

"Did you call Mr. Weiner?"

"No," she said. "I was in a fog. I couldn't think. Numb." But she did recall that she went back into the bedroom several times, "hoping for a miracle, that it's not true." But Colleen Harris also told the court "I knew he was gone. He would be okay."

In the space of several sentences, the term "fog" had appeared twice. But judging by the conversation in the lobby during breaks, the defendant's testimony was starting to clear things up.

Alexander wanted to know how long after she realized Bob was dead she took his coin collection to San Francisco.

"Quite a while," she said. She was "wandering around in daze" but saw the coins, which filled two large bins. And she recalled that Bob had another collection of colored quarters in a glass case.

"All I could think about was protecting the coin collection," she told the court. The house would be vulnerable after her arrest and "I finally decided San Francisco was the best place to take them," the residence of Wesley Thornberry.

Meanwhile, "I knew half his head was blown off," the defendant said of Bob Harris. "Of course, I knew I would be arrested. I saw his head." But "I don't know what took place. How it took place."

Colleen Harris again described the scene with the police, dogs, lights and "guns pointed at me." The jury had heard this before. After she became aware again, Joe Alexander wanted to know, how long it took to pack up the coins.

"I don't know how long."

Alexander asked how long was it before she left for San Francisco?

"I don't know."

Alexander produced a record of a cell phone call to Wesley at 7:26 on Sunday morning, the next day. The defendant said she left a voice mail that she was coming. She was "pretty sure" there was nothing in the call about the coins.

Harris said she returned to the bedroom several times but didn't move anything. After returning from San Francisco, Alexander wanted to know, did she wipe part of the bedroom ceiling?

"Yes," she said. But during the time when she was "in a fog" she did not clean up the bedroom. She recalled the "blow" and Alexander asked if this blow had been the result of a shotgun going off.

"That's all I can think," she said.

Alexander then raised a point that had been missing from his questions the previous week. The Boito side-by-side double-barreled 12-guage shotgun her father allegedly purchased from Kmart in San Pablo is not a high-end weapon like a Beretta or Benelli. All the same, it shoots powerful 12-gauge shells, and one doesn't want to stand in front of it at any time. As Colleen Harris had observed, it packed sufficient force to leave part of Bob Harris on the ceiling. The blast from that weapon, with its shortened barrels, would make a huge noise easily heard over great distance.

"Did you hear anything?" Alexander said.

"No."

"Did you hear the shotgun go off?"

"No."

That response elicited no audible response in the courtroom's still crowded gallery. The stately Alexander paused briefly before continuing.

He cited a 9:41 a.m. call in Wesley's neighborhood and asked about Bob's cell phone, which the defendant said he was "always losing." She wasn't sure whether Bob's phone was in the box with the coins and Bob's .22 revolver. It emerged that Jim Batten's gun was also a .22 revolver, but with a larger frame. Colleen testified that she left Bob's gun in a brown paper bag with the coins, and she acknowledged that other tenants had access to Wesley's garage. For Alexander, that raised a point.

Andy Harris, Bob's son, lives in Colfax, not far from Placerville, and much closer than San Francisco, a drive of several hours. Why not take Bob's coins and guns there?

"Wesley was the first to pop into my head," she said.

Alexander named several people the defense had advanced as character witnesses. Did the defendant know any well enough to trust them with the coins?

"No," she said.

Alexander asked Colleen Harris if she took a shower before she left for San Francisco.

"No."

"Did you have blood spatter on you?"

"I don't know if I did nor not."

Alexander cited several calls but the defendant shed no light on a missing span of an hour and a half.

"I don't remember," she said. "I'm not making it up. My head was in a million places. I was really distraught." But she told the court that she was not going to give the coins to the police or to Andy Harris.

At 2:51 p.m. on Sunday, January 6, 2013, someone placed a call from Colleen's home phone to the residence of David Weiner, and the call had lasted six minutes and 56 seconds. Alexander asked if she remember that call.

"I left a message," Harris said. "We did not speak directly." But he did call back, she said, and the two spoke. Then he came to the house and the two spoke in his car. This went on for "quite a while," Harris said. "I was going through deep emotional things." She had been to the bedroom and told the court Bob hadn't moved, nothing had changed and "I didn't know what to do."

Alexander asked if she and Weiner had talked for 90 minutes.

"I have no concept of the time at all," she said.

"Did you give him anything?"

"No."

The prosecutor asked if she told Weiner what to tell 911.

"No."

Did she move Bob? Alexander asked.

"I went into the bedroom and lay next to him," she said. "I held him for a while. I straightened up. I just waited."

"Did you move the covers?"

"Yes."

"Did you move Bob?"

The defendant said she untangled his legs.

Alexander asked if she moved the gun.

"I pushed the gun out of the way," she said.

"Did you wipe the gun down?"

"No."

"Is this also the time when you wiped the ceiling?"

"Yes," she said. When laying with him and talking to him, "I looked up and saw stuff hanging from the ceiling. I didn't want the kids to see that."

"Did you move his arm?"

"I didn't want to lie on top of it," she said. "I did move it." But she told the court she didn't know if Bob's left arm was tucked under his head when she turned on the light. In her account, she moved nothing else of Bob's, and this was all before she met with David Weiner in the driveway.

During this testimony David Weiner was slowly rocking back and forth as Alexander honed in with his questions.

"When you lay down next to Bob, were you wearing clothes you wore when arrested?"

"Not the jacket."

"Pants?"

"No."

"Did you change after lying next to Bob?"

"I was going to end my life."

"You were going to kill yourself?"

"It was all my fault."

"After you laid down with Bob," Alexander said, "did you change your clothes?"

When she lay down with Bob, she said, "I had underpants on."

"What did you do when waiting for police to arrive?"

Harris told the court she made sure the house was in order, and put some important papers in a brown ceramic jug. The deputies saw her do that, and she had no doubt about their testimony. Harris had told the dispatch operator, her first contact with law enforcement after the death of Bob Harris, that all was okay.

"Things were not okay," Alexander said, as he continued.

The dispatcher had asked: "Did you hurt somebody?"

"I can't talk right now," Harris had responded. "I knew I wasn't supposed to talk. I didn't know why."

An officer asked: "Did you shoot your husband?"

"Maybe I shouldn't answer that," she responded. And in the interview with detectives Mike Lensing and Paul Hadjes she was "in and out" though she did say she saw a little blood on the pillow and thought it was a nosebleed. Alexander asked why she didn't tell them more.

"It didn't come into my head," Colleen Harris said. The detectives asked about the calls she made but "I was in a fog, not knowing what I had done." Dr. Tresser, she said, "helped me open up" and the memory of the calls came back "over time."

The fog was back, along with Dr. Tresser. Despite his help, Miss Harris didn't recall requesting that dispatchers send no ambulance because Bob wouldn't like that.

"He was dead," she told the court.

Alexander noted that in 1985 she had requested no sirens. Harris said she was not worried about sirens in 2013.

"His death was between the two of you?" Alexander said.

"I was the only one there."

Harris told the detectives she had no prior memory problems.

"I did say that," she said.

But she had no memory of the 1986 trial? Alexander wanted to know.

"Absolutely none," Colleen Harris told the court, adding, "I have no memory of the time Bob was killed."

Alexander noted the memory lapses over Bob Harris, Jim Batten, and the 1986 trial. Were these, he asked, the only three such lapses in her life?

"I would have to see," she said.

"All three involve death of your husband?"

The defendant said that as far she knew, she had been alone with Jim Batten. But with the detectives in 2013 she forgot that she met with David Weiner. Alexander asked the date when her memory returned. She couldn't pin down an exact day, but Harris said she "assumed" that Dr. Tresser was working with Weiner.

"I had a lot on my mind," the defendant said, when speaking with the detectives, and did not tell them that she had been arrested for Batten's murder.

"I didn't understand why he was being brought into the picture," she said. She had wiped out memories of that case, but didn't tell the detectives anything about it.

"Your inability to remember only relates to what makes you look bad?" Alexander said.

"No," Harris responded.

Harris told the court she had denied climbing up on the countertop, and did not know if the 1986 prosecutor possessed her journals. She did tell the detectives she performed surveying work for David Weiner, and after the murder trial worked for him as a paralegal. Yet, she forgot that Weiner had represented her in the 1986 trial. On other matters, her memory was clear.

"A lot of married men have made advances on me," she said. But Larry Dodge, she said, had "15 affairs" in their seven years of marriage. She didn't know about Jim Batten's affair "until after." And that, she said, "totally blew me away."

Even so, she told detectives, "I'm not hung up about somebody sleeping with somebody."

"Did you know Bob was dead when talking to detectives?" Alexander said.

"Yes," she said. "I didn't want it to happen."

She didn't tell the detectives about lying next to Bob, or say that Bob had committed suicide. But in her journal, she wrote, "If I had a gun I'd blow my head off."

Harris didn't tell the detectives Bob was killed by accident and told them she never touched the gun. In court that day she said "I wasn't sure what had happened" but she felt the gun and moved it. "I just pushed it with palm of my hand," she said.

Joe Alexander spent some time on the defendant's divorce and remarriage to Bob Harris for the purpose of getting Jim Batten's Social Security benefits. She said she "never got a dime," from Larry Dodge beyond child support.

Alexander outlined a trust Bob Harris established in 1990 that left Colleen a 1961 Austin Healey Sprite, a 2004 Ford Escape, along with a boat and trailer. The trust also left her the dividends from Bob's investment portfolio, $733,317 in securities, and more than $60,000 in cash.

"I was in shock to see how much money I had in there," Harris said, but "I didn't hack the computer for investments" before Bob was dead.

The trust, established on August 31, 1990, left everything to her, and the benefits lasted as long as the other lived. Bob was now dead and Joe Alexander asked Colleen about any injuries she had after Bob had been killed. Turned out she had one on the inside of the right middle finger.

The bailiff brought in a long cardboard box, from which Alexander extracted the double-barreled shotgun, people's exhibit number 11. Alexander asked Harris if she knew the shotgun has a trigger guard.

"It probably does," she said.

Alexander demonstrated that, with most of the stock cut off, the weapon would be very difficult to fire from the shoulder in the usual manner, as she would have done with the 30/30 when killing the elk in Montana. Harris said she only went elk hunting "one time."

Alexander asked if the elk she killed was a bull or a cow.

"A bull," she said with no hesitation. The bull elk was so big that to bring it home she had to cut the animal into four pieces. It was wintertime, she said, and she wrapped the meat and put it in the snow because they had no freezer at the time.

"Have you ever fired a shotgun?" Alexander said.

"No."

Alexander asked the defendant if the gun now in court was the one that killed Bob Harris.

"Yes," she said.

"The truth is, Miss Harris, you were holding the gun when Bob was killed."

"I guess I was," she said.

"You went in with this gun and held it to the back of his head and pulled the trigger."

"I did no such thing."

"And that gun went off and blew off the front of Bob's face."

"I did not do that."

"I pointed a gun at them."

On April 8 the rains had abated but it was still on the chilly side in Placerville, where some passing cars bore thick caps of snow. The pro-victim and pro-defendant factions huddled out front of the courthouse, waiting for the doors to open at 8.

The session was slow to start and the new faces in the crowded gallery included Colleen Harris' grandchildren. Before nine the judge appeared.

"Bring her in," bailiff Scott Crawford said.

Colleen Harris entered in the familiar pale pink blazer with the large bow on the front, above the waistline. It was the same outfit she had worn on opening day, and a throwback all the way to 1985.

David Weiner had more questions for Harris but the first witness was attorney Thomas R. Van Noord, a tall man in a gray suit. He told the court he practices family law and civil litigation from an office in the same suit as Weiner's, but testified that the two had "no business relationship." Van Noord also told the court he represented Colleen Harris in three matters.

The children of Robert Harris had filed a wrongful death lawsuit against the defendant, and he represented her in that. One of the plaintiffs, Pamela Stirling, had filed the suit, and Van Noord had filed the denial. Discovery had been stayed because of the present criminal proceedings.

Van Noord also told the court that his client was the beneficiary of the Harris trust. Colleen Harris' civil attorney pegged the value of Mr. Harris' estate at $1,083,000. This included a value of $275,000 on the Lake Tahoe house, which he said still carried an outstanding loan.

Deputy District Attorney Joe Alexander asked if Mr. Harris had more than enough money to pay off the debt.

"Yes," Van Noord told the court.

Alexander turned his attention to Colleen Harris.

"If acquitted, would she have a claim to Bob Harris estate?"

"Yes, she's a beneficiary."

Alexander asked what she would get. Van Noord said Colleen would get the use of the Tahoe property and possessions, all the vehicles other than the MGB, and the checking account.

"Would she also get interest from stocks?"

"Yes," Van Noord said, but the attorney could not peg an annual figure.

Joe Alexander also asked Van Noord if he had ever represented Colleen Harris before.

"I may have," the attorney said.

Alexander found the answer a bit vague. He asked Van Noord if it would surprise him to know that he appeared in Harris' prior murder case. That did not entirely settle the matter.

"If I appeared," he said. "It was on Mr. Weiner's behalf."

As the transcript of the 1985 preliminary hearing confirms, Mr. Van Noord did represent Colleen Batten on behalf of "her attorney of record" David Weiner.

Judge Melikian excused Van Noord and Colleen Harris again took the stand. David Weiner asked her how big Larry Dodge was.

"Six foot five."

In the incident with Dodge some 42 years ago, Weiner asked, "you had a gun?"

"Yes."

"Did you have him arrested?"

"Yes, he was arrested."

Weiner did not present any records of this arrest, but asked about any damage Dodge had inflicted. Colleen Harris said she still has scars around her left eyebrow.

"How did he inflict that damage?"

"With his hand," she said. "Punching." Harris said this happened when she was standing and on the ground.

"When you held the gun," Weiner said. "Did you point it at him?"

"I pointed it at him," said Harris. And after this incident she took the children and headed back to California. She told the court she later wrote about the incident in her journal, and never hid it from Bob Harris.

Attorney David Weiner then recalled the incident with Harris's second husband Jim Batten. Had she faced him with a gun in hand?

"Yes," Harris said.

"Did he move on?"

"He jumped off the couch and ran to door," said Harris, who told the court, "I never hid that from anybody."

Weiner asked about legal issues after Batten's "death."

She said they owed money on 10 acres in Cool, another foothill town. And Harris said she got calls threatening to sue her for the jobs Jim Batten had started but not finished. There were some 50 of these, she told the court, and it took two years to clear them up.

"I was basically in the hole," she told the court.

"How did you meet me first?" Weiner asked.

Harris said it was through the issue with her daughter in 1979, and that she did not know Weiner before that time. He asked if she had gained anything from any insurance policy Batten had taken out.

"No," she said.

Weiner asked about gains from any insurance policy on Bob Harris' life.

"No," she said, and she didn't know what had happened to the sterling set, a gaming table, and an Austin Healey sports car.

Weiner asked about the last journal entry at Lake Tahoe, where she wrote that if she had a gun, she would blow her own head off. At that point, she said, she believed it was over with Bob and she was "devastated" and "shocked" about his affair. The jury had heard all this before at considerable length. Weiner recalled testimony of her standing on a countertop to put documents in a vase.

"I got a step stool," she said. She had not stood on the countertop, she said, but may have had her knees on it.

Judge Melikian called for a break and soon the lobby was buzzing again. Over by the stairway, one photo of an old judge came loose and had to be taken down. Several others hung crooked and the drinking fountains on both floors still bore "out of order" signs.

After the break, before the jury returned, the issue of psychiatrist Dr. Norman Tresser surfaced again. Weiner had told the court he had suffered a stroke and was unable to testify, but he had spent 25 hours with Colleen Harris, and this counseling had taken place after the death of Robert Harris and before the current trial. Colleen Harris said that the psychiatrist "helped me to be able to verbalize what was going on in my head." She said "everything was confused" and "a lot of grief" along with "fog," a term now familiar to the court.

Joe Alexander noted that Colleen Harris had already blurted out Tresser's name, not in response to a question, and in violation of a court order not to do so. This, the Deputy District Attorney said, was for the purpose of "ringing the bell" with the jury and was an "implied expert opinion" plucked from the 1986 trial. Alexander objected that Dr. Tresser was not available for him to cross-examine, and this invited speculation from the jury.

Weiner countered that his client had "serious memory issues" and was "not trying to fool anybody." Judge Melikian reviewed the record and noted that Colleen Harris had indeed been the first to mention Tresser. He had the name stricken and said the questions to Harris on this subject would be limited to what had already been asked. If she added more, the judge told the defendant, he would hold her in contempt.

After consultations with court reporter Michelle Tuttle, Weiner went through the same questions. Tresser, it turned out, had provided 25 hours of assistance and helped her verbalize what was going on inside her head.

"What was going on in your head?" Weiner asked.

"I was trying to remember exactly what took place," she said. On that theme, some clarification remained.

Weiner asked her about the 2003 declaration charging that she "pulled a gun" on Larry Dodge and Jim Batten.

"I pointed a gun at them," she said. "I didn't pull a gun." So in her attorney's view, the 2003 statement that she never "pulled" a gun on anyone was true. She had only "pointed" the gun. That dubious distinction had some in the gallery shaking their heads, but Judge Melikian took no action.

Weiner turned to the bedroom scene with Robert Harris. There she felt the first blow in "my belly area" and the second on the chest, the one that left a bruise.

"I had a feeling it was probably the gun," she said.

Weiner asked Colleen how much she weighed."

"108, 110," she said.

And Bob Harris"

"205, I think," she said, referring to his "size 40 pants."

When she received the blows, Weiner asked, was she wrestling with Bob?

"No."

"How could he move you off his back?"

"All I know is he flung me over."

Joe Alexander asked the defendant if the blow to the chest was the one "like a sledgehammer," as she had previously testified.

"Correct," said Harris, who told the court "It was there and I was shuffling it around. To get it away from me." She recalled "groppeling" with her husband. Alexander asked if this meant she was fighting for control of the weapon? On this point the long hours with Dr. Tresser yielded little clarity.

"I can't really say," she said. "I didn't want it near me" and she was still "grappeling with it."

Alexander asked if Bob was resisting.

"I don't know," she said. "Bob threw me off. It happened quickly."

After some questions about Wesley, whom Colleen Harris had given power of attorney, Alexander asked when Bob Harris found the shotgun. The defendant said this had been between March and June of 2012. So he knew about the gun which, Alexander said, was "capable of blowing your head off." And the defendant acknowledged that Bob intended to stay in the Placerville home.

Alexander briefly raised the divorce and Social Security matter and asked if Bob got an inheritance from his father, Tom.

"I think he did," the defendant said.

Alexander asked if she was upset that she got nothing from this inheritance.

"No," she said. "Absolutely not."

Alexander swung back to the scene in the bedroom, with the recoil of the gun that had struck her in the chest.

"Was Bob killed as result of an accident?"

"Yes."

"It was not suicide?"

"No," Colleen Harris said.

The defendant acknowledged that Bob, as the DA put it, "had positive things going on." He played cribbage, umpired baseball, golfed and skied with his kids and their families. Then Alexander asked:

"It is not your claim that you shot Bob, pulled that trigger, in self defense?"

"No," Miss Harris said, with no hesitation, contradicting what her defenders had claimed before the trial started.

After some questions on Jim Batten's Social Security matter, which brought Colleen $1,100 a month, David Weiner also returned to the bedroom scene.

"Did you have any intent of harming Robert when grappling with the gun?"

"No," she told the court. "I wanted to spend rest of my life with him."

Weiner raised the prospect of danger from the weapon.

"I wanted the gun out of the picture," she said. "I was not thinking about harm."

"Did you intend to kill him?"

"Absolutely not," the petite, pink-clad woman told the court. "He's been the love of my life."

Alexander asked Harris how old she was when James Batten was killed.

"I don't know," she said. "Do the math."

It emerged that at the time she was in her forties and not eligible for Social Security benefits. Back then, she said, "I never thought about it."

Alexander, meanwhile, called the person she talked to when she did think about it.

Angela Johnson, clad in a light purple sweater, told the court that before retirement she worked for the Social Security Administration and her husband Lance was Bob Harris' cousin. She knew Bob for 30 years and Colleen for 25 years. Around 2004, Colleen contacted her about getting Jim Batten's survivor benefits. Johnson explained that these were payable after age 60, that she had to have been married at the time of death, and unmarried when she filed for the benefits. Colleen asked about the divorce matter. She could keep the benefits if she remarried. She wanted to do this, Johnson said, because Jim Batten's benefits were "higher than her own." And Bob was a federal employee, who did not pay into Social Security.

Alexander asked if Colleen had raised the issue of Bob's inheritance.

"Yes," said Johnson. "She was disappointed that Tom had not left her something." And she was also disappointed that "Bob had not transferred some to her," for the same reason. Colleen felt she had been a good daughter-in-law.

Weiner expressed some surprise that this matter had been provided to him in discovery. He asked Johnson when she learned about the divorce.

"After his death," she said. John had talked to the prosecution's investigator Joe Ramsey, who inquired about the relationship between Bob and Colleen.

Alexander asked the witness if she had been truthful with the investigator, and in court.

"Yes," Johnson said.

Alexander then recalled Dr. Gregory Reiber, the forensic pathologist who had performed the autopsy on Robert Harris. At Alexander's request, Reiber offered a detailed explanation of rigor mortis, a change in the muscles after death. Rigor starts almost immediately and full rigor can take place in eight to ten hours. It can be broken, the pathologist said, but "will never reform to any degree."

Alexander asked Reiber if he had found anything unusual about the body of Robert Harris, a man of moderate build. The shotgun wound had caused too much damage to tell anything about the jaw, but the left arm was "held by rigor." After eight to ten hours, the doctor said, it would have been "probably impossible" to stretch it out. If the attempt had been made at 1:30 the next day, it would have been possible, but only with great effort. And the left arm would have remained supple, which was not how the doctor found it. Based on his testimony, if someone had moved Bob Harris' left arm, they would have to have done so in the first couple of hours after the shotgun blast killed him.

Harris' weight had been estimated at 205 but in Dr. Reiber's report he weighed 182 pounds. Alexander asked if that might reflect blood and tissue loss from death. The doctor agreed.

Alexander then called Karen Hodges, a woman who had served as an accountant for the Tahoe Baikal Institute from 2004 to 2012. She was unaware that Bob had used TBI funds for his Mongolia trips, and she testified that he made attempts to reimburse TBI for meals. He took no salary and volunteered his time. Hodges told David Weiner that Bob Harris "never took money," and that she "never funded a ticket for him."

Hodges was the last witness of the day. Judge Melikian told the jury to return the following Tuesday, and by the end of that day they might begin deliberations. Weiner was ready to rest his case and Alexander had only a couple of witnesses, including Brian Black, former husband of Tawnie Black.

The jury filed out but Melikian remained on the bench to resolve questions about jury instructions. Someone asked whether a certain witness would be asked to tell the truth. Off the record, Melikian said, "We don't ask people to tell the truth. We tell them."

"The physical evidence does not lie."

On April 14, crews were still working all night on Main Street until 8 a.m. when the El Dorado County courthouse opened its doors. Reporters and spectators packed into the gallery and saw Colleen Harris enter in the pale pink outfit with the large bow in front. Joe Alexander opted for a dark suit and bright reddish tie. Judge Melikian started promptly and Alexander called witness Brian Black, a bespectacled, balding man with a heavily lined face. He told the court he was Tawnie's fourth husband and had been married to her from April 1992 to January 2011. Before their divorce the couple had two children, born in 1996 and 2002, but the witness had been brought in on another matter.

Joe Alexander recalled Tawnie's 2003 sworn declaration in quest of a restraining order. This was the document in which Colleen told Tawnie that if she was not such a slut, none of this would happened, but Alexander did not cite the line that day. Brian Black said he was aware of the declaration but gave no advice to Tawnie, did not help write it, and did not even read it. Tawnie Black was not present in court that day, but she became the subject of testimony. There had been a "falling out" between Tawnie and her mother.

"Her mom and her did not see eye-to-eye on what happened to her daughter in her younger years," Brian Black told the court. He had been present at a meeting between Tawnie and her mother Colleen several months before the declaration, in which they tried to "iron out" the issues.

"Tawnie did not feel like her mom validated her feelings, what

183

happened to her," Brian Black told the court, and "Tawnie was trying to process this for several years."

Under questioning from David Weiner, Black said he didn't know that Colleen was concerned about her daughter.

"Tawnie was very angry," Brian Black said. "She was not getting answers from her mom," but did not consult a psychiatrist.

Alexander called detective Mike Lensing, who told the court he had been present on the first search of the Wilderness Court property on January 6, 2013, which carried over into the next day. They got new information and came back the next day.

"She mentioned a safe in the interview, and I did not remember seeing one," Lensing said. But on January 8, in one of the closets, the police found a safe measuring two by three feet. New information prompted another search on January 9 and detective Lensing said they found "a hiding spot that Colleen Harris had used in the past." The secret spot was in the attic above the pantry and accessed through the bedroom. They did not find the cell phone or diaries there, but in the course of entry did notice a Windex bottle.

Under questioning from Weiner, Lensing revealed that phone records revealed Colleen Harris' course of travel. The police found her diaries in a filing cabinet, and one on the counter was not hidden.

Joe Ramsey, the DA's investigator who had been sitting with Alexander throughout the trial, told the court it took him one hour and 10 minutes to drive from where Colleen Harris had made the AAA call and her Wilderness Court residence. On January 9 Ramsey had been part of the search for Colleen Harris' personal effects, including her wallet, but the gray Toyota Camry in the garage yielded nothing. Her personal effects, Ramsey told the court, had yet to be recovered. Ramsey also testified that the house, though left secure, had been burglarized and ransacked, with items strewn about and a brass bird left in the driveway.

This was the first mention of such a burglary and recalled Weiner's testimony on the 1985 burglary of his client's house while she had been in jail. The attorney had not told the court that his client had discovered the 1985 burglary while out on bail, and that the only missing items had been computers. In the current case, Weiner's client had been denied bail and remained in jail. So who, exactly, had burgled a house where a murder had taken place, a house draped with yellow crime-scene tape, and where police had made repeated visits, remained something of a mystery.

David Weiner then called Wesley Thornberry, who told the court he had also seen the brass bird in the driveway. Thornberry said there had been "some disagreements" about how to distribute Bob's things. Weiner asked Thornberry if someone at the Mongol Ecology Center had tried to fire Bob Harris. That drew an objection from Alexander, which Judge Melikian sustained.

Under questioning from Alexander, Thornberry said he delivered two boxes of coins to Weiner, but no cell phone. The witness recalled the note from his mother to give the collection to Bob's family, but testified that he did not follow the directions and gave the collection to his mother's criminal defense attorney. Bob Harris' gun he found on a different occasion, after he returned to San Francisco, and after his mother's arraignment. On January 6, David Weiner had called Thornberry about the arrest. According to Thornberry, the division of Bob's property was amicable for the most part. But he said he never saw the elusive cell phone in any of the boxes.

That closed out the witnesses and the court admitted no more evidence. Judge Melikian then reminded the jury that the defendant was being tried for murder under section 187. That meant acting with malice aforethought and without justification. The judge told the jurors they had to decide if the killing was unlawful. He mentioned the issue of "brandishing a firearm" but told them not to consider evidence from the 1985 shooting. After lunch, Joe Alexander delivered his closing arguments.

Colleen Harris shot Bob Harris, "because she loved him" and "obsessed that she was going to lose him," as she had documented in her journal. The night that Bob was shot and killed, the defendant entered the bedroom as Bob lay sleeping. She aimed a shotgun behind his left ear. She held gun in front of her, "put her finger on the trigger and pulled the trigger."

Alexander again produced the double-barreled shotgun and explained the bruise and injury from the trigger guard. With its cut-off stock, the gun was very difficult to shoulder.

"That's the most basic part," said Alexander, who proceeded with the aid of a screen demonstration. The motive involved a marriage on the rocks, the affair with another woman, Aza. Bob was not communicating his plans. The means involved the shotgun and she "knows where the murder weapon is" and how to use it. Then came opportunity. "Bob was asleep in bed when he was killed, or resting." He was "unconcerned and unaware of what's happening around him."

He sustained a "non-contact wound," so this was not a suicide. Rather, it showed the "state of mind of the person pulling the trigger." That person knew that if the muzzle of the gun touched Bob, he would wake up.

"The physical evidence does not lie," Alexander said. "It does not change its story. It does not forget. It does not have bias." Bob was asleep or at rest when killed, not fighting or struggling with the gun, and of this there was proof beyond a reasonable doubt. The physical evidence is subject to interpretation but the jury, "can't base reasonable doubt on what is unreasonable."

Alexander walked the jury through the crime scene, with Bob lying in the position in which he was killed and the multicolored blanket with "an even pattern of high-velocity ammo" and blood spatter evidence. He was shot behind the left ear, "the shot went out the front of his face," and this was "inconsistent with struggle."

The shotgun was "remarkably clean," with no transfer of spatter. But there were "smear patterns on the ceiling," which meant that someone had attempted to clean it up.

"The crime scene had been altered," Alexander said. "Suicides don't alter crime scenes and killings by accident don't do that." As Dr. Reiber had demonstrated, it was "impossible" for this to have been a self-inflicted gunshot wound.

At the time of the autopsy the whole body was in "full rigor" and after two to three hours Bob is "not moving." He was shot and killed after 8:23 p.m. and before 7:26 a.m. the next day, which marked the beginning of the defendant's trip to San Francisco. Even if moderate rigor had been broken it would have been obvious. The defendant said she got back in bed with the victim and moved his left arm. She said this was after the visit with Weiner, then she changed it to before because she had to match Dr. Reiber's testimony.

The defendant's story, Alexander said, was "completely inconsistent with physical evidence." If she had cleaned the ceiling when she returned from San Francisco, the blood spatter would have dried in the seven hours she was gone. The change in her story, Alexander said, was her "attempt to run between the raindrops, the evidence."

To find reasonable doubt, the jury would have to conclude that the defendant is truthful and reliable. The jury, he said, should consider if she is lying, and if she no longer remembers something, and whether that was inconsistent with her earlier statements on the subject. And was she evasive? The jury could consider that "the tears were false or fake, for effect." The defendant, "couldn't answer, so she changed her answer."

In his seat beside the defendant, David Weiner was slowly rocking back and forth as Alexander continued.

The defendant, "denies something that later turns out to be 100 percent true," the deputy DA said. "She's picking and choosing what to remember, what she can lie about," and "for reasonable doubt, the defendant's case has to be reasonable."

Alexander recalled the defendant pulling a gun on Larry Dodge and Jim Batten. She showed "selective amnesia," describing in detail incidents in Montana yet claiming she remembers nothing about the 1986 trial, even though in the current case she told detectives she had been a "murder defendant."

By claiming she was in a "gray fog," Alexander said, "She's avoiding the problem. She has to lie. She doesn't know what lie to tell, until she knows more about the investigation." Therefore, said Alexander, "selective amnesia is false amnesia. It is a lie."

It was "pitch black" in the bedroom, the defendant had testified, yet she noticed that Bob had a "nosebleed," not the "massive wound in Bob's head." David Weiner came to the house and the two talked for 90 minutes before the 911 call went out. She said she wasn't on the countertop, but officers saw her there. She had changed her story many times, Alexander told the jury and, "If you are telling the truth you don't need to do that." The defendant will "say whatever she can to fit her story" and her behavior was an issue.

She said she took the coins to San Francisco because she knew she would be arrested and the house would be vulnerable to burglars. Yet she put them in a garage where all tenants would have access. And during the interview with detectives she was "evasive, misleading and untruthful."

Alexander also noted "adoptive admissions," such as her response to the dispatcher's question whether she hurt somebody. "I can't talk right now," she said.

And when asked if she shot him, she had replied, "maybe I shouldn't answer that." In fact, Alexander said, "she knew Bob was dead."

The business about being "in a fog," Alexander told the jury, was "an excuse for a 24-hour period she didn't want to talk about." He recalled the "goal-driven behavior" of driving to San Francisco, recalling key codes, and calling AAA.

"She's not in a fog," Alexander said. "Everything she's doing has a purpose" and her behavior was "the exact opposite of being in a fog." She called her defense attorney, not 911 or and ambulance. The fog, said Alexander, is "an updated version of 'I don't remember.'"

Alexander reminded the jury that Tawnie Black was a defense witness, and that the defense then changed and discredited her testimony. Tawnie had been doing everything to help her mom when "the daughter" was challenged about the restraining order. The defendant used what happened with the daughter "to create a false narrative," that she killed a man who was raping her daughter. Yet the sexual assault only came out in the earlier trial, not in interviews with the police.

Alexander's points of motive, means, and opportunity had been emblazoned on the large screen to the jury's right, and in plain view of the defendant, her attorney, and the gallery. The court now saw words adapted from the 2002 Shasta County case of the people versus Steele, that when the same person does the same thing in same place, the more reasonable it is that such an act is intentional. And "the more often one kills, especially under similar circumstances, the more reasonable the inference the killing was intended and premeditated." Alexander then outlined the similarities.

In 1985, Colleen and Jim Batten had marital issues, and those were also present in 2013. In 1985 there was another woman, who turned out to be "the daughter," and in 2013 it was Aza, in Mongolia. In 1985 and 2013 a woman had been in the room when her husband was killed. Both cases featured memory problems, with claims of a gap in memory as part of the defense. In 1985 and 2013 there had been a delay in the reporting of the crime, and in both cases "a new story at trial." Money issues were also present both times.

"I must prove that the similarities are true" Alexander told the jury.

He found false narratives in the money issues and the defendant's effort to "paint Bob in a bad light." And he asked the jury to consider the defendant's tone of voice and demeanor on the AAA call.

"She knows Bob is dead and when she killed him." Alexander said. "She's animated. She gave her phone and answered questions," and she was "not grief stricken or suicidal." If she had been suicidal, "would Weiner leave her with a dead husband and a loaded gun?" The defendant, "takes piece of truth and uses it to tell a lie."

She described being in bed with Bob, naked and under the covers, and rubbing his neck. In that account, "he was turned away from her." So her story about how Bob died was not credible and "none of it makes sense." She took a sledgehammer blow, called it "an accident" and "she comes to then see that Bob is dead." There was no evidence that it had happened this way, Alexander said, "just the defendant's claim that she was in a fog." The notion that she covered Bob with a blanket because was sick with bronchitis and had a nosebleed was a "colossal lie."

The gun, in fact, "knocked her for a loop," then she put the brown blanket on top of the multicolored blanket, after she had shot Bob. Here too she had "adjusted" the story, claiming that now there was enough light, after pitch black.

The defendant claimed that the call to David Weiner was just a message on his machine, but "she had to have told him Bob was dead." When asked how he learned that, Weiner said he got a phone call. The defendant claimed to be moving valuables and "doesn't want you to think she's writing a check to Mr. Weiner."

The defense, Alexander said, had an obligation to present evidence supporting its case, and the jury could consider their failure to do so. They could have called many experts on the memory issue, the deputy DA said, but chose not to. As he explained, for a manslaughter conviction, Colleen Harris must first be found not guilty of murder. First-degree murder involves malice aforethought and killing without lawful excuse or justification. That she took a gun, pointed it at Bob and pulled the trigger, Alexander said, was "evidence of intent to kill," and if he failed to prove that, it was second-degree murder. But shooting while someone was asleep or relaxed was the very definition of "lying in wait," and striking from a position of advantage. And that she made the decision beforehand, Alexander said, was obvious.

"Pointing any gun at someone's head is a decision," Alexander said, "everything she did shows intent to kill," so manslaughter did not apply. "The defendant had motive, means and opportunity. She knew where the gun was and shot and killed her husband."

Alexander's statement recalled what his fellow El Dorado County prosecutor Lisette Suder said in the same courtroom during the Winkler case, before the same judge, Kenneth Melikian. Defendant Todd Winkler had "two dead wives."

Defendant Colleen Harris had two dead husbands.

"Look at the similarities," Suder told the jury. "He is the only witness."

Likewise, Colleen Harris was the only witness in the present case.

Suder urged the jury to "Look at the wounds. That is the evidence, ladies and gentlemen."

Alexander had invoked the fatal wounds Bob Harris had suffered. That was evidence against his wife Colleen Harris.

Alexander told the jurors they were "the finders of fact in this case." And they should find that Colleen Harris was "guilty of murder," he said, "guilty of murder in the first degree."

David Weiner objected that Alexander had used the propensity argument and called for a mistrial. Judge Melikian disagreed, noting that the prior act has to be similar, and the deputy DA had pointed that out. If Weiner wished, he would repeat certain instructions to the jury but the trial would proceed with Weiner's closing arguments the next day.

"She killed Bob Harris."

April 15, the deadline to file tax returns, dawned clear and bright in the Sierra foothills. Inside the courthouse, Colleen Harris had switched back to her magenta outfit and wore her hair in a long braid. In the crowded gallery, between Debbie Munro and Wesley Thornberry, sat Melody Weiner, David's wife, dressed elegantly in black. In the same courthouse where he had gained acquittal for the same client in 1986, David Weiner delivered his closing statement to the El Dorado County jury. The attorney had doubtless pondered it long and hard, but he did not get off to a good start.

In the early going he referred to "Mrs. Harris," who was not married, and a tacit reminder that her husband Bob Harris had in fact been killed, the reason for the current proceedings. Weiner quickly shifted to "Miss Harris," and thanked members of the jury "for giving up part of your lives to be here." The attorney said he would start with the prosecution's case theory.

"May I have that shotgun?" he said.

The bailiff brought in the weapon in the long cardboard box and Weiner took it out. With its shortened barrel and stock, the double-barreled shotgun looked menacing as ever. For many in the courtroom, it was an odd tactic to bring in the shotgun his client had acknowledged holding at the crime scene.

The prosecution, Weiner explained, charged that the crime was pre-planned and that Colleen Harris had been lying in wait while Robert Harris slept with his hands behind his head.

"She takes a gun," Weiner said, "bends over and blows part of his head off, killing him."

The courtroom remained quiet, but the jury, prosecution and gallery alike might have wondered why the defense attorney had repeated those gruesome details. As he had explained after losing the Winkler murder case, the "gruesome stuff" had worked against him. And there was more to come.

"I'd like to talk to you about a drop of blood," he said, showing a photo with Bob Harris left hand on his chest and a drop of blood on the left index finger.

The multicolored blanket over Bob Harris had an "even spray of high-velocity blood splatter," what he also called a "fine mist of blood splatter." But "where is that on the hand?" Weiner said. "That puts us back to what Miss Harris described" and "the evidence tells the story." Weiner displayed crime-scene photos as he narrated the story. He noted "where the shot goes into just below the ear." The "wound was huge" and "came out in the area of the upper face."

"Take a look at the angles," Weiner said. "It goes in by the ear and does a U-turn?" The shot, he said, had come from "someone much lower, who is fumbling with the gun when it goes off."

Weiner told the jury "we know that Colleen Harris is involved" and recalled her finger injury, her experience with guns, and the bruise on her chest. That, Weiner said, "does not occur in preplanned event. That occurs because of an accident." It was an accident, he said, "and something that happens on the spur of the moment."

As Weiner had it, "obviously, there are things happening simultaneously. She's getting hit from another direction, and conscious when the trigger was pulled." Therefore "our position is that it's an accident."

At the hospital, Colleen reported no chest pains. "She's numb from what happened from seeing her husband of 22 years, whom she loved dearly, with his head blown off."

In the space of several minutes Weiner had twice described the victim with his "head blown off." The graphic language drew no audible response from the gallery and the jury listened carefully as Weiner continued.

Robert slams the door but the "submissive wife" climbs into bed to massage his neck and back as she apologizes. Then, "She becomes aware of something that turns out to be this gun." This upsets her and "things race through her head." She wonders "if he is going to hurt me." Bob curses her, and flips her off of him with his left hand. Then he "takes the gun and slams that into her body. She then grapples with it, under the covers, and that thing goes off." The muzzle had to be outside of the covers and the gun is three to six inches from his neck, "maybe a foot," Weiner said. It is "much more consistent that the barrel is parallel with the bed than someone shooting down" and the "head may have been at different angle, moved over by force of blow," which Weiner, citing the prosecution's firearms expert, said packed 2,000 pounds of force.

"That's how she says it happened," Weiner said, "and the evidence supports that, as opposed to someone lying in wait."

"She," Colleen Harris, was the one on trial, but Weiner had plenty to say about Bob Harris before his head was blown off. He was "extremely distraught" and concerned about "his image and reputation" and his "path to self-destruction." He had told Pam Stirling that "this old body is really falling apart," and Dr. Reiber found he had an enlarged heart, high blood pressure, diabetes, several surgeries, elbow and knee implants, gum problems and other ailments. He's "not happy about what's happening with his body" and also "this thing that's going on with Aza."

Weiner backed his client's claim that she never pulled a gun on anyone but recalled how she had used her "right to use a gun to protect herself and others." First husband Larry Dodge "had been beating on a two-year-old," and with "Mr. child molester," Jim Batten, she got the gun from a drawer and "doesn't pull it from any hiding place." Therefore, she "didn't lie" and "she never pulled a gun in any of those instances."

Weiner then shifted back to Bob Harris, "a good man, a bright guy, educated, an achiever," who "did well in our society." He had been married and it failed and his "image is precious to him." Bob the environmentalist "got fired from MEC," and "there goes his legacy." He was stressed and "will be considered a phony and a fraud."

As Weiner spun it, "he's got a good thing going" with the situation in Mongolia but owes about $200,000 on the Lake Tahoe cabin. His "dutiful wife was standing up on her own hind legs," Weiner said, and on January 5, 2013, Bob was worried that he would lose the cabin, Colleen's income and "his cook, his gardener." And he will lose out on the move to Hawaii, which is "2,000 miles closer to Mongolia."

Meanwhile, Colleen was still "madly in love with him," but traumatized when "all of a sudden his head is blown apart right next to her." That made three times David Weiner had explained in graphic fashion what had happened to Bob Harris. She was "full of grief and despair," Weiner said, but "we know she has a history of memory loss."

Even so, she "took the coin collection where it would be safe" and again showed herself a subservient wife. "She is loyal to Robert, doing his bidding, what he wants." She has a nursing background and "she knows he's dead" but can't let the children "see this." So she cleans up, and "tries to wipe off flesh hanging from the ceiling." She makes the bed, Weiner said, and this creates problems for law enforcement.

Detectives Roberts and Lensing note her shock and reality disconnect, her flat effect. She remains in a "gray fog" and "numb." Weiner told the jury that this was not an amnesia case but "she has difficulties talking about things," though 25 hours with Dr. Tresser "helps her immensely." The attorney did not specify what, exactly, Dr. Tresser had immensely helped the defendant to do.

Weiner recalled that in 1985 his client had testified that James Batten held a gun to her head as he forced her to perform oral sex while telling her that her daughter did it better. In the current case, the attorney said, Tawnie had been "used to try to make her mother look bad."

Weiner dealt briefly with the issue of the cell phone before returning to the shotgun, which he opened and held aloft. At the time of the crime, one barrel had been fired and the other had an unfired shell. Now both barrels had debris, he said, before returning to the "spot of blood" on the victim's hand, where the prosecution's expert said that fine mist would be.

"It was an accident," Weiner told the jury. "Find that true." Under cross-examination, his client had said "It's all my fault. She takes the blame for it. It wouldn't have happened if she hadn't violated Bob's directive on Aza. If she hadn't, Robert wouldn't be dead. Does that sound like she's hiding from you?"

Weiner told the jury "you are the finders of the truth" with an abiding conviction of truth of charges, "otherwise you must acquit."

"Good luck," he told the jury. It was a rather odd statement to a body assigned to assess facts and evidence in a homicide. Such matters are hardly a roll of the dice but "good luck" was not Weiner's last word.

He told the jury he had misstated the law. If it was an accident, he said, "then that's the end of it."

Weiner returned to his seat beside Colleen Harris. The courtroom remained quiet, and Judge Melikian directed Joe Alexander to begin his rebuttal. The burden of proof was his, so Alexander had the last word.

Reasonable doubt, he told the jury, "has to be based on something reasonable," and Weiner was asking them to speculate by finding truth in the testimony of the defendant, and everything about what Bob Harris is like is from her. Dr. Tresser was not able to testify but the defense could have brought "many other experts" on the memory issue. "They chose not to."

As for the shotgun, the California Department of Justice had fired it in tests, which left residue in the barrels, so Mr. Weiner was asking for speculation on that too. As for the "subservient wife," Alexander recalled the defendant's own testimony in which she was not subservient. In the case of Larry Dodge "she got a gun and called the cops." With Jim Batten, she "gets a gun and chases him out of the house." So the subservient wife, Alexander said was part of "a false narrative."

The defendant's cell phone went missing after the AAA call and was "still missing." People don't put their cell phones in the attic "or where it won't be found." This was a "good example how the defense tries to run between the raindrops." It was "made up on the fly in response to evidence." And Alexander took aim at Weiner's key theory.

"This case is not about one drop of blood," Alexander said. "It's about a thousand drops."

The deputy DA reviewed what detectives had said, corroborated by Dr. Reiber's testimony on rigor mortis. The evidence showed that Bob Harris was not expecting the shot. The notion that he was fighting over the gun yet turned his head away was "preposterous," Alexander said.

He then recalled the defendant's statement to Tawnie Black that she could "fool any counselor," and the jury now knew from Brian Black that he had not forced Tawnie into that declaration. The jury also knew "how the defendant is involved" in the death of Robert Harris, and her claim that she doesn't remember was "a strategy to avoid responsibility."

"The case is yours now," Alexander told the jury. "Go back there and do the right thing. Hold her responsible. She put her finger on the trigger, and she killed Bob Harris."

Alexander sat down and Judge Melikian repeated what he had said earlier about the 1985 case, in which Colleen Batten was acquitted. Similarity or lack of similarity could be considered but it could not be used to show that the defendant had a bad character or was predisposed to commit crime. After some final instructions, the jury went "back there," but they didn't stay long.

The jury had heard Colleen Harris tell the story, at considerable length. They had seen her one-woman show, with the weeping scene, another repeat performance of 1986. That jury had bought it, but this group seemed aware that nothing weeps more readily than a block of ice. And these jurors recognized that her testimony had, in effect, transformed the witness stand into the Liar's Bench bar just down Main Street. This time, Dr. Norman Tresser's vaunted "psychogenic amnesia" emerged as Colleen's Disease, an affliction that makes someone want to forget they are a murderer. For their part, members of the jury were not forgetting what they had heard in the courtroom. And despite Mr. Weiner's instruction, they were not relying on luck.

In less than an hour, about the time it takes to fill out the forms and complete the procedure, the jury ruled that Colleen Harris was guilty of first-degree murder.

In the courtroom, magenta-clad Grandma Cokey shielded her face and cried. She made no statement but her attorney David Weiner told reporters "she took it hard, hard, hard," and that she was "distraught." By her own account, she had considerable experiences with such feelings. For relatives of the victims the ruling brought some relief. Bob's son Andy Harris told reporters the defendant had lied many times, and "It was really hard to sit through that." But "in the end, it all worked out."

"I wish the jury could have heard how wonderful he was," a tearful Pam Stirling told Peter Hecht of the *Sacramento Bee*. "I think justice served will be a good start for our family to recover from this tragedy." Stirling also told the reporter that "my dad was very unhappy in the marriage and wanted out." The Los Angeles detective then stated a truth that had been particularly obvious to observers of the trial.

"When someone wants to break away from another person," Stirling said, "it seems that the other person can make a decision other than to kill him."

The post-verdict silence in the media also proved notable. Those who previously wondered how "a woman so small in stature" could murder her husband were nowhere to be found in news stories. Neither was Jennifer Mouzis, the defense attorney who had held forth about abusive husbands and threatened wives. The stories were also missing quotes from Paul Laufman, the 1986 jury foreman, and the neighbors who didn't want to rush to judgment. That judgment was now in.

As Joe Alexander said, Colleen Harris put her finger on the trigger and killed Bob Harris. That story made national news in January 2013, and when the 2015 trial started. But on April 15, 2015, not a single television camera showed up and the major crime story of the day was the conviction of former New England Patriots football player Aaron Hernandez on charges of murder, and his sentence to life imprisonment.

For her part, Colleen Ann Harris, also known as Grandma Cokey, was staring down the barrel of 50 years to life. Judge Melikian set the sentencing for June 5. In the meantime, the convicted murderer would have more to say.

"I don't belong in prison."

"During the course of the investigation," El Dorado County probation officer Angela Hastings noted in her report, "many people interviewed stated Colleen commonly either lied or embellished stories." She did that in her trial testimony, and after being found guilty continued to lie and embellish in her May 7, 2015 statement for the probation report. For example, under the heading "Circumstances of the offense," she wrote, by hand, in block letters:

"I was married for 22 years to a very troubled man who I loved with all my heart, a man who after retiring was completely lost, a man so desperate to be in the limelight, who's image to the world was of paramount importance and whose private life was kept in utmost secrecy." He was "leading a double life" but "I knew I still loved Bob and cared deeply enough to hang in there."

On New Year's Eve, 2012, "I finally felt we were truly healing." The couple "laughed together and even snuggled and cuddled for the first time since his return" from Mongolia. "From this moment until January fifth life felt good." They even talked about moving to Hawaii but "then in a split second life made a radical change."

The last sentence recalled a scene from the 1979 film *Kramer vs. Kramer*. Attorney John Shaughnessy (Howard Duff) asks Joanna Kramer (Meryl Streep) if she was a failure at the single most important relationship in her life.

"It did not succeed," she says.

"Not 'it,' Mrs. Kramer," the attorney responds. "Were *you* a failure…"

In this case, "life" did not made a radical change. Rather, Colleen Harris made a radical decision to kill her husband in a way that hideously disfigured the man.

Under the heading "Why you committed the crime," the convicted murderer wrote:

"What happened to my partner was a horrible tragedy, a horrible accident I never saw coming." The district attorney "twisted and distorted the truth to present an image he wished the jurors to believe that I was somehow this evil, jealous mom." And the DA portrayed her daughter as "the other woman" in her life. "How cruel and sick is that," wrote the convicted murderess.

"I never layed in wait for Jim or for Bob. Their deaths were never planned. I don't know why things happened as they did with one partner deciding to put a gun to my head and then pulling the trigger and the other partner taking a gun to bed. I have no answers. The only thing I know for sure is that I <u>never</u> planned their deaths with God as my witness."

The phrase "how cruel and sick is that" would stand out to police, prosecutors, and particularly to the relatives of the victims. In light of events, it took a special kind of person to write something like that.

Under the heading "Your feelings about your present situation," the convicted murderer wrote:

"I have spent my entire life trying to be the best wife, mother, daughter, stepmom and citizen that I could possibly be. I believe very strongly in the Ten Commandments and God's teachings and have lived my life accordingly. I have never drank, used drugs, smoked, swore or even drank coffee. I have never stolen, never missed a payment on anything. I have never applied for welfare even when there were times when I was struggling. I guess my biggest problems were being too caring, too forgiving, too willing to turn the other cheek and being too willing to accept the blame for things that went wrong, in order to keep peace and harmony."

It had evidently escaped the notice of the defendant, who according to her closest friend had read the Bible four times, that one of the Ten Commandments says "you shall not murder." So to that crime the defendant had now added religious hypocrisy.

Under the heading "Why you should be granted probation, if permitted by law" the convicted murderer wrote "my husband's death was a horrible accident" and offered a prayer.

"Heavenly Father: help guide us to know that the value of life is measure by the moment spent with you, learning to give of ourselves, sharing your wisdom, inspiring hope, wiping tears and touching souls," and so forth. "I am not a bad person" and "being locked in a box, surrounded by so much anger, hate, drugs, deviant behavior of unbelievable magnitude is beyond my comprehension.

"I can't believe this is what God wants. I don't belong in prison. I am not guilty. My husband's death was a terrible accident." She concluded: "My children and grandchildren need me and love me and I need and love them. Locking me away has forever damaged so many lives in so many ways."

Probation officials duly noted the enlistment of God in the cause. They also took note of what the convicted murderess had not written.

"In her lengthy statement," Angela Hastings wrote, "the defendant does not express any concern for, or recognition of what the victim's sons and daughters are going through."

Those sons and daughters would soon get their chance to tell the court exactly what they had been going though.

"She killed him, didn't she?"

On June 5, 2015, it was heating up in Placerville, and not much going on at the old El Dorado County Courthouse with the Civil War cannon out front. During the noon break, reporters, a television cameraman, and the familiar relatives and friends of Bob Harris began to arrive. Most of Colleen Harris' friends seemed to have abandoned her, and the no-shows included Debbie, Wesley and Tawnie. Their mother entered the courtroom through the side door to the jury room, not the front as before. The magenta and pink outfits had given way to a bright orange jail jumpsuit over a white long-sleeved undershirt. In this outfit she looked small, but not what Pat Lakey had called "petite" in 1986. The convicted murderer sat at the table the prosecution had occupied during the jury trial, near the jury box and looking away from the gallery. Her attorney David Weiner wore a light gray suit and seemed rather subdued.

When the time came to present the defense motion for a mistrial, it was Erik Schlueter, not Weiner, who made the case. The goateed attorney argued that Alexander's use of the Steele case constituted propensity. The DA's argument, Schlueter said, "went down the slippery slope and stepped on the mine."

Judge Melikian encouraged the attorney to carry on at any length he needed, and listened patiently as he stated the same argument in several ways. Alexander, Schlueter said, had "stepped over the line."

Alexander, now sitting nearer the judge, countered that he had not done so. He had followed the law, stayed within the bounds the judge had outlined, and therefore, he said, the motion should be denied. Judge Melikian duly denied the motion. When he asked Weiner if there was any reason the judgment should not be pronounced, the attorney said no, but he did raise a complaint about the probation report, contesting the accuracy of the defendant's statement. Judge Melikian rejected the complaint, then turned to Colleen Harris.

This was the woman who had testified for two days and written a seven-page statement of nearly 2,000 words in the probation report. At the direction of her attorney, who as in 1986 had put her on the stand, she now had nothing to say, not a single word. But she did turn and look back toward the gallery, face rigid and her mouth a straight line. The children of Bob Harris would now have their say.

From a podium at the front of the gallery, Andy Harris' wife Michelle read a statement from Karen Harris, the victim's first wife. It saddened her to see her children "hearing so many lies told of their father and not be able to respond." Bob's five grandchildren, ages 9 to 23, she said, will "never again have their grandfather join them" for birthdays, sporting events.

"Their world has changed and they were forced to grow up so much faster by losing their grandpa who they loved very much by such a senseless and mean-spirited tragedy."

Joe Alexander then took the podium to read a statement submitted by Scott Robert Harris, the victim's youngest child, who was not present.

"Robert Harris was a loving father. He will be missed in too many ways to count." Scott and his father did not always agree on matters of faith and politics, the statement said, but "I wanted to see what other changes in perspective might occur, during the later years of his life. Because of the defendant, I will miss out on that too.

"The murder of my father was a disgusting act, utterly self-centered and selfish. The shooting was a personal decision by the defendant, but the consequences have rippled through the lives of hundreds of people who knew and respected my dad as a father, brother, grandfather, uncle, cousin, friend, co-worker, environmentalist, umpire, parishioner, and volunteer. I am one of the many people who felt his loss greatly, and will continue to feel it, for years and decades to come."

Nobody in the courtroom could doubt it.

Andy Harris, the victim's oldest son, had brought a photo of his father and stood it on Joe Alexander's desk facing Judge Melikian. Andy had brought a lengthy prepared statement but decided to set it aside and improvise. He had heard his father demeaned as lazy, selfish and out to bilk money from an organization. And he wasted little time setting the record straight.

"My dad was a great man," Andy told the court. "You would have liked him." He was not unskilled and could repair anything. He had rebuilt a 1958 bug-eyed Sprite. He was a master gardener, and "not a lazy man." A contributor to society, Andy told the court, he had umpired thousands of games, for no payment at all. That's why "hundreds" had showed up at his funeral.

Andy said his father had a "good marriage for a long time." He "loved Colleen's kids as his own," even though "they said hateful and mean things to my dad." Andy said he had talked to his dad three days before he was killed. He was planning to see Scott's daughter play baseball. He "never thought of suicide" and "had so much to live for," recalling that his own father had lived to 96. Andy "never saw him handle a gun" and his father "never manhandled a woman."

As Colleen turned to look back, Andy said, "There is no doubt in my mind the defendant maliciously, hatefully, shot my dad while he was sleeping." She did this because she "couldn't stand that he was leaving."

"Who does that?" he said. "Who shoots somebody sleeping? Who shoots their husband?"

The trial had answered those questions, which Andy's written statement addressed. Colleen could have let Scott's father leave and go back to his lake Tahoe house, just as he had planned.

"This is what normal people do," the statement said. "Instead, the defendant acted maliciously and selfishly. She crossed the line without regard for the pain it would inflict on me, my family, and my dad's friends. The defendant should receive the maximum sentence for murdering my Dad in cold blood. She should be shown no mercy, especially in light of the evidence that came to bear during this trial about the murder of her second husband, Jim Batten, which proved the defendant killed Jim Batten in cold blood." Perhaps as part of God's plan, Andy told the court, "this case brings justice for Jim Batten's murder, justice that the defendant escaped two decades ago through lies and manipulation as the evidence showed."

Andy Harris did not know Jim Batten, but he had clearly surmised that there was more to the man than what the defendant, Tawnie Black, and David Weiner said about him in court.

By imposing the maximum sentence, Andy told the court, "You will be honoring my Dad, a man you would have loved to meet and would never forget, and you will be giving our family a greater sense of closure knowing the defendant will never get out of jail – a sense that I hope and pray one day will bring an end to the pain we have had to endure and still are enduring."

Andy took his seat but his words lingered in the courtroom. If his paternal grandfather had lived to 96, his father Bob, just into his 70s, surely had miles to go before he slept, as Robert Frost put it.

Pam Stirling, clad in a white blouse and black skirt, moved to the podium. Like others in the courtroom, the LAPD detective had been keeping her emotions in check with some difficulty. Unlike her brother Andy, she stuck to her written statement.

"Let me first go back and describe to you the worst day of my life. It was the morning of Monday, January 7, 2013, when my boss called me into his office where my close friend stood crying."

June 5, 2015, marked nearly two and a half years since that day, but Pam Stirling told the court she had not forgotten.

"I asked if my children were okay. Was my husband okay? The concern on their distraught faces was evident when they told me it was not my kids or my husband. A gut-wrenching fear engulfed my body as I asked.

"It's my dad. She killed him, didn't she? I just knew."

Pam Stirling thanked the prosecution and jurors for seeing through the "appalling lies" and "following the abundance of evidence that overwhelmingly proved the defendant is a cold-hearted murderer." And the trial, she told the court, confirmed that the defendant "also murdered her second husband James Batten."

After the verdict, Pamela Stirling said she wished the jury could have heard how wonderful her father was. The jury was gone, but Bob's daughter would tell the story.

"I always start describing dad by how smart he was. He knew

something about everything. He was a solid and grounded gentleman. He was kind and he was honest. My dad was a jokester who enjoyed a good laugh. My dad was a humble man who could make you feel at ease. He was very social, and loved talking with people. I admired how he could enter a room, and before the event was over, he had spoken to every single person in attendance. He had a passion for life and making other people's lives better."

Her dad, Stirling said, was "a giver, not a taker." When she asked advice, "he gave me the truth of what I needed to hear. He was a good man. This is the man the defendant stole from us." And "the horrible parental lesson the defendant leaves behind, her legacy, is 'if someone wants to break up with you, murder them.'"

Stirling told the court "I do not forgive the defendant. That is for God to do, and if I could, I would likely encourage Him to do otherwise." She concluded: "We encourage and support the maximum sentence, along with a lifelong sentence of unending sorrow, grief, sadness, heartache and void that we wake up to every day."

During the trial, Judge Melikian had cautioned the gallery not to show responses to testimony. But as he listened to the impact statements, the judge himself showed some emotion. He told the court the evidence in the case was overwhelming and none of the defense's claimed errors, even if they had occurred, would have changed the trial. There would have been no hung jury, the judge said, and "nothing but guilty." And the judge had reached the same decision as the jury.

Echoing the probation report, he said Colleen Harris wanted to avoid prison and showed, "no concern or sympathy for the victim's family." Said the judge, "In all my years as a practicing trial attorney, and my six years as a judge, I have seen very few acts more selfish or self-centered than that in this case."

For many who had been through the trial, the judge's statement, though welcome, probably understated the matter. "Selfish" and "self-centered" are terms suited for a petulant child or egotistical teenager. Judge Melikian doubtless could have broadened his description, but he hadn't showed up that day to make speeches. He was there to hand out a sentence. He gave Miss Colleen Harris, also known as "Grandma Cokey," 50 years to life, a de-facto life term. And Melikian also pronounced sentence on the murder weapon. The shotgun, he said, "will be declared a nuisance and be disposed of."

The judge extended condolences to the Harris family, then adjourned the proceedings. In the lobby, the Harris family members comforted one another and talked to reporters. It was some time before the orange-clad defendant emerged, and she stepped quickly into the elevator as Nikons clattered. The door closed and she was gone.

The hills around Placerville were alive, but not with the sound of silence.

On June 24, 2015, Colleen Ann Harris left El Dorado County Jail to become inmate WF2509 at the Central California Women's Facility (CCWF), also known as Chowchilla. To be considered for parole, she would have to live past the age of 120, so prison is likely the last stop for the convicted murderer. That arrangement is perfectly fine with LAPD detective Pamela Stirling, daughter of Robert Edward Harris, forest ranger, umpire and Grandpa Big Bear. And Freida Batten also approved.

"I find it a satisfying thought," said Freida, "that her grim and nearly hopeless incarceration in ghastly Chowchilla is her punishment for Jim's death."

Freida Batten, an opera aficionado of great erudition, never got to make a victim impact statement in 1986. In 2015 she had some thoughts on her former husband Jim Batten, surveyor, outdoorsman, survival trainer, and "the best of the Air Force," as the Scout leader told his commander way back in 1959.

"He was a good man and he was a worthy man," Freida said. "He was worthy of respect. He worked hard all his life and deserved an old age to enjoy. And she took it away from him."

Yes, she did. She got herself a shotgun, loaded it up, and killed Jim Batten before he could run. Had she not done so, Jim would still be in his 70s, sharing memories with his nephews and playing golf with friends. He used to tell Freida they might get together again some day. She never took that seriously, but in the fullness of time a reunion of sorts did take place. On February 21, 2016, Freida Lee Batten passed away at the age of 73. She lived to see Jim Batten's killer sentenced to prison, then reunited with him in death.

When Judge Melikian pronounced sentence on June 5, 2015, he reminded David Weiner to file an appeal, and the attorney did so on June 11. In this action, Weiner had the full support of his client.

"I will appeal," Colleen Harris wrote in the probation report, "but I'm 73 years old and the cost and time involved are a deep concern." She also wrote, "I don't belong in prison. I am not guilty. My husband's death was a terrible accident." She also asked "Is there anything I can do outside of waiting for my appeal to be considered? My children and grandchildren need me and love me and I need and love them. Locking me away has forever damaged so many lives in so many ways."

At this point, costs and time were the least of her concerns. The others had been settled in a full and fair jury trial, in which she had been represented by the same attorney who gained her acquittal on murder charges in 1986. Her husband's death was not a terrible accident. She killed him, just as she killed Jim Batten. She did belong in prison, which is where the state sends convicted murderers. As it turned out, there was nothing she could do while waiting for her appeal.

On June 6, 2016, a year and a day since Judge Melikian sentenced Colleen Harris, the Third District Appellate Court denied her appeal and upheld the judgment against her. So inmate WF2509 will remain in Chowchilla, where, as she wrote in the probation report, she will be "surrounded by so much anger, hate, drugs, deviant behavior of unbelievable magnitude." But maybe another convicted murderer, perhaps a younger woman, will take a shine to her and offer protection.

When Colleen Batten got away with the murder of Jim Batten in 1986 she gained control of his assets. She gunned down Bob Harris for similar reasons in 2013, but this time the victim's family would take the matter to court. On June 20, 2016, two weeks after the appeal court upheld her sentence, the civil trial would begin in Sacramento.

Thomas Van Noord, one of her attorneys in the 1986 trial, had been representing the convicted murderer in the civil action, but on February 26, 2016, Colleen Harris fired Van Noord and began representing herself. She did not appear in El Dorado Superior Court on June 20, 2016, and as at the sentencing, neither did Tawnie, Debbie and Wesley. On the other hand, Bob Harris' sons Andy and Scott appeared, and so did Bob's first wife Karen and his best friend Gary McCormick. Several witnesses testified, including detective Mike Lensing, but unlike the criminal trial, the proceedings would wrap that same day.

The court found in favor of Bob Harris' family, awarding $4.5 million in damages plus $1.5 million in punitive damages. Shortly after that judgment, rumors began to circulate that Jim Batten and Bob Harris might not have been the only victims of inmate WF2509. For those who knew her best, those rumors could not be easily dismissed.

As the criminal trial confirmed, women are equally capable of murder as men. A woman who gets away with murder is likely to kill again. And the more often she kills, in similar circumstances, the more likely the act is intentional and premeditated. Around Placerville, at least one writer was already investigating the possibilities.

Acknowledgements

The author thanks Pamela Stirling and Phillip Stirling for their kind cooperation during a painful time in their lives. Thanks to Freida Batten, Terry Stone, Diane Neal-Barrett and Michael Bowker for background on Jim Batten and photographic materials. Christy Lillie and Joe Alexander of the El Dorado County District Attorney's office never failed to show courtesy and professionalism. Thanks are also due to Rosalie Tucker, Melissa Thompson and Michelle Tuttle of El Dorado Superior Court. The archives of the El Dorado County Library proved invaluable, and Cole Mayer of the *Mountain Democrat* compared notes on trial testimony. In all cases, thanks for the help. Responsibility for the content of this book is mine alone.

For Further Reading: Other Books by Lloyd Billingsley

Readers of *Shotgun Weddings* might consider the author's *Exceptional Depravity: Dan Who Likes Dark and Double Murder in Davis, California.* Reviewers said:

"A thought-provoking, fast-paced page turner, which fans of crime stories are sure to enjoy."

"Mr. Billingsley's meticulous historical research and accessible writing style makes for compulsive reading. It's the perfect book for fans of history and crime stories. One note of caution: don't start reading unless you have lots of time because you won't be able to stop until the last page."

"Seldom does a writer capture both the human drama and legal maneuvering in a criminal trial. Billingsley does both with wit and a clear vision."

Readers of *Shotgun Weddings* might also like the author's *Hollywood Party: Stalinist Adventures in the American Movie Industry.* As Academy Award winning actor Charlton Heston said:

"Mr. Billingsley's book is the best exploration of the Hollywood blacklist and the Communist Party's role in that conflict."

Herb Romerstein, co-author of *Stalin's Secret Agents*, said:

"Mr. Billingsley's tells the story of the battle for the soul of Hollywood."

www.ingramcontent.com/pod-product-compliance
Lightning Source LLC
LaVergne TN
LVHW011226080426
835509LV00005B/342